150 TIMELESS MOVIES

PRAISE FOR *150 TIMELESS MOVIES*

"...lways trust Susan Granger to steer me to the movies I'll love (as well as the stinkers ...). Not only is she a good guide, but she's a fun read. I am honored to be included ...timeless 150!"

—Keir Dullea, actor, star of *2001: A Space Odyssey*

"...san Granger is a true Hollywood insider. Her father was a director from Hollywood's ...len age, her mother a leading socialite in the film industry crowd, her son is one of ...ay's bright studio executives, and Susan herself is a passionate and tireless syndicated film critic and writer who is read daily on websites and in newspapers around the world. No one knows more about movies, old and new, and the way the film world works than Susan. So what an immense treat it is to have her for the first time talk about 150 of the movies that have intrigued her most within the covers of one book. It all makes her new book, *150 Timeless Movies,* **something I recommend to anyone who loves movies as much as Susan Granger and I do.**"

—Robert Osborne, prime time host of *Turner Classic Movies*

"Susan Granger and I swam in the same Hollywood waters when we were growing up (my father was Gary Cooper). Motion pictures and all that encompasses are in her DNA and she is a rare critic who knows the industry from the inside. She brings her judgement of "hits and misses" tempered by knowledge, good taste and a sense of respect for what good movies can be and do for their viewing public. Susan Granger has given us this guide, *150 Timeless Movies*, which should be an important addition to the library of anyone who loves film. Bravo - and thank you!"

—Maria Cooper Janis, actor Gary Cooper's daughter

"I have known Susan since she was four years old. She was bright then—she's even brighter now—in every way. And she knows how to separate the wheat from the chaff."

—actress Jane Powell

150 TIMELESS MOVIES

SUSAN GRANGER

Hannacroix Creek Books, Inc.
Stamford, Connecticut

Editor's Note: Reviews found in this book are a combination of reprinted selected reviews from the author's website, http://www.susangranger.com, which has close to 3,000 reviews, as well as more than two dozen original reviews of older classic movies, and an Introduction, written by author Susan Granger exclusively for this book.

Published by:
Hannacroix Creek Books, Inc.
1127 High Ridge Road, #110
Stamford, Connecticut 06905 USA
http://www.hannacroixcreekbooks.com
hannacroix@aol.com

ISBN: 978-1-938998-75-1 (hardcover)
       978-1-938998-76-8 (trade paperback)

Library of Congress Control Number: 2016952847

CONTENTS

FOREWORD

Jill Schary Robinson
Author, *Bed/Time/Story*, and daughter of Dore Schary,
Former MGM Head of Production

usan Granger and I grew up together in the film world. We'd sit in projection rooms listening to our fathers discussing dailies and rushes with the best editors, writers and directors of the "Golden Years." Even as a kid, Susan watched movies with a clear perspective. She was never snowed by glamour. She always knew what she saw, what she really thought, and she had the courage to tell you. Susan saw first-hand the conflicts, hard work, diligence, and commitment it takes to turn a great story into a film which will reach deep into people's hearts; a film which has, as our fathers called it, "the motor" which transforms an audience.

She is the ultimate insider who approaches each movie with enthusiasm, energy, and intrigue. But despite all Susan's experience, she has never become aloof, bitter, or cynical. Her reviews are smart, clear, witty, and utterly reliable. You read a Susan Granger review and you'll know why you will want to see this picture (or why you *won't*).

Reading *150 Timeless Movies* is like settling in for a remarkable evening at the movies with your best and smartest friend. Just heat up some popcorn and have a completely delicious time.

Issued

Branch: Dublin City Rathmines
Date: 9/06/2022   Time: 2:30 P
Name: Lewis, Eugene

ITEM(S)	DUE DAT
50 timeless movies	30 Jun 202
XPL200000712	

Your current loan(s): 2
Your current reservation(s): 0
Your current active request(s): 0

To renew your items please log onto My
account at https://dublincity.spydus.i
Thank you for using your local library

INTRODUCTION

Once upon a time there was a magical land called Hollywood. It was mythical, but nobody knew it. Not even we who were there. I was born in Hollywood. Not in a trunk, like Judy Garland, but in Cedars of Lebanon Hospital. Since I was born at noon, my father, director/producer S. Sylvan Simon, was able to be with my mother in the hospital for my birth before returning to the set later in the afternoon.

With Lassie in *Son of Lassie* (1945)

Back then, Hollywood was a one-industry town. My father made movies like *All the King's Men* and *Born Yesterday*. As a child, I was fortunate to be able to play small, bit parts in movies.

In costume with parents on set of *Bad Bascomb* (1946) which starred Margaret O'Brien and Wallace Beery, directed by my father, S. Sylvan Simon

My father died while he was preparing *From Here to Eternity*. When my mother remarried, she chose an M.G.M. producer, Armand Deutsch.

Later, after studying journalism with Pierre Salinger (before he served as Press Secretary to President John F. Kennedy's), I became a radio and TV newswoman. Eventually, I became a movie critic, a job I've held for more than 30 years. During that time, the motion picture business has moved from analog to digital, and movies that used to be seen only in theaters are now viewed in a multiplicity of forms.

But this book isn't about me. For more than a century, Hollywood has shaped our dreams, our aspirations, and our heroes. Entertainment has become one of the United States' leading export. Our films and television reach virtually every corner of the world. Movies change the way we think. They shape how we view ourselves, each other, and the world around us.

From the beginning, Hollywood influenced business. Back in 1934, when Clark Gable emerged bare-chested in *It Happened One Night*, the undershirt industry died. In *E.T.*, Reese's Pieces candy enticed the lovable alien out of hiding, giving birth to the product placement industry. Former actor Ronald Reagan became president of SAG (Screen Actors Guild), government of California, and was twice elected President of the United States.

While *Webster's Dictionary* defines "timeless" as "eternal or ageless", it's perhaps audacious to apply that to a medium that is barely over 100 years old. While movies were, undoubtedly, the most popular art form of the 20th century, they're also an easily visible archive of our history. And the perennial question facing moviemakers is: should movies try to influence their audience or simply reflect the society of their time?

There's no question that movies do influence us, in ways that are both mundane and profound. They're a chronicle of fashion, style, and speech, offering idealized visions of life that audiences yearn for. Their persuasive logic can sway our thinking on morality or war or history.

Creating entertainment is a diverse and highly competitive industry. That's why it's called show business, rather than show art. When a motion picture actually transcends its profit intent, it's often considered miraculous.

In 1871, Horace Greeley is quoted as advocating, "Go West, young man," and Hollywood created the cowboy mythology, beginning with Thomas Edison's *Great Train Robbery* (1903), the first Western ever made. Its closing image, a bandit pointing a gun at the audience and firing, terrified people so much they ran out into the street.

Over the years, we've discovered that movies deliver both knowledge and articulated ideas. That's what makes them vital to our society and culture. We yearn to cross the transom of our social universe and enter the lives of people we'd never meet in our own neighborhood. Psychiatrist Carl Jung said, "The cinema, like a good detective story, makes it possible to experience without danger all the excitement, passion and desire we must suppress in ordinary daily life." Silent film movie star Lillian Gish once called Hollywood "an emotional Detroit, where you buy a catharsis instead of a car." Pablo Picasso commented, "Art is a lie that enables us to realize the truth."

While the branches of the Academy of Motion Picture Arts and Sciences acknowledge the various elements that go into a successful movie—writing, directing, acting, cinematography, sound, and so forth—a good director can elevate a generic plot, and a great story can be torpedoed by lackluster execution.

I believe the 150 movies that I've chosen for this collection of reviews, many of which have been made since the turn of the 21st century, yet still including 25 classics, will stand the test of time. It's ironic that the downfall of numerous contemporary films is their reliance on a special-effect technology that tends to obliterate story-telling because, essentially, movies are visual storytelling. They are a form of entertainment. Although we can now view these films on personal computers, movie-going is, at its core, a shared, social experience.

Perhaps what makes these movies timeless is that they were unforgettable the first time they were viewed. They were new and exciting, many movies reflecting a different set of values and mores. But our collective memory is generational. Some people forget very quickly, and young people often don't seem to care about the past at all, which is itself a mistake. If you don't know where you've been, how do you know where you're going?

Thomas Edison once said, "I consider that the greatest mission of the motion picture is first to make people happy – and to bring more joy and cheer and wholesome good will into this world of ours. And God knows we need it."

Timeless movies come in all forms: animated, comedy, drama, horror, romance, war, western, documentary and science-fiction. What they all have in common is that they're a successful creative collaboration, often revolving around love, family, and the indomitable human spirit.

Susan Granger

150 TIMELESS MOVIES

Contemporary and Classics, English and Foreign Languages

2001: A Space Odyssey (M.G.M.) (1968)

Stanley Kubrick's visionary sci-fi epic fantasy revolves around an extraterrestrial black monolith. This mystical object is first seen at the Dawn of Man in a barren landscape during the Pleistocene era. A simian-like Moon-Watcher touches it and discovers the first tool, transforming him into a predator.

Then the perfectly rectangular, massive slab catapults into the 21st century, as a vehicle docks within the hub of a gigantic, rotating spaceport, discharging its only passenger, scientist Heywood Floyd (William Sylvester), on a top-secret visit to America's moon-base. His assignment is to investigate a second monolith that's been excavated in a crater. When Floyd reaches out to touch the pillar, it emits a piercing, earsplitting shriek that sends the explorer reeling.

Cut to the spaceship Discovery with its crew of six: mission commander Dave Bowman (Keir Dullea), executive office Frank Poole (Gary Lockwood), and three others in suspended animation. A computer named HAL 9000 (courteously voiced by Douglas Rain) monitors every function of the mission toward a third monolith that's orbiting Jupiter. When peevish HAL suddenly expresses paranoid misgivings, Bowman and Poole think HAL's judgment is deteriorating, so they discuss disconnecting the computer's consciousness centers as rebellious HAL attempts to outwit them. Finally, there's a hallucinatory star-gate into outer space and beyond—with Bowman is reborn as an angelic, symbiotic fetus Keir Dullea headed toward cosmic destiny.

With an intellectually audacious, psychologically dense script by Kubrick and Arthur C. Clarke, based Clarke's short story, "The Sentinel," its metaphysical theme explores human evolution— where we came from, where we are and where we're headed—with serenely visual imagery by cinematographers Geoffrey Unsworth and John Alcott and Oscar-winning special effects. Similarities are obvious between the majestic slab and the enigmatic plinths of Stonehenge and the Cyclopean statuary of Easter Island.

On the Granger Movie Gauge of 1 to 10, *2001: A Space Odyssey* is a trippy 10, epitomizing the archetypal voyeuristic, audiovisual experience, consistent with the 1968 psychedelic delirium of a drug-oriented, computer-dominated society engaged in nationalistic competition with Russia for Cold War dominance in space exploration.

3:10 to Yuma (Lionsgate) (2007)

No one knows how many thousands of Westerns have been made, but the first notable one was *The Great Train Robbery* in 1903. Since then, we've watched Westerns for more years than there was a Wild West, since they're usually set in the years between the conclusion of the Civil War and the end of the 19th century.

James Mangold's re-make of Delmer Daves' 1957 anti-hero redemption saga revolves around the psychological conflict between a crippled, courageous rancher, Dan Evans (Christian Bale), and a notorious killer, Ben Wade (Russell Crowe). After suffering a period of draught and subsequent debt, Evans' family is awakened one night to discover their barn burning and small herd of cattle rustled, subsequently serving as a stampede diversion for a stagecoach robbery. That sets up his first encounter with Ben Wade—but far from his last.

Writers Michael Brandt and Derek Haas have added to Elmore Leonard's story and Halsted Welles' original script, making it more violent, cynical and brutal—with the clock-ticking convention of *High Noon* and *Rio Bravo* and an enigmatic conclusion. James Mangold (*Walk the Line*) keeps the tension taut as Evans is grimly determined to deposit Wade on the 3:10 train to Yuma prison.

Russell Crowe's sophisticated, multi-dimensional sociopath anchors the story, while scowling Christian Bale's seems weighted down with stoic, stubborn, idealistic virtue. Or perhaps it's just his choice to underplay. As Wade's dastardly accomplice, Ben Foster scores, and Peter Fonda is memorable as a corrupt bounty hunter. On the other hand, the 'frontier women' (Gretchen Mol, Vinessa Shaw) are too creamed and coiffed to be even remotely believable.

On the Granger Movie Gauge of 1 to 10, *3:10 to Yuma* is a gritty, galloping 8, an authentic Western with cynical, contemporary touches.

8 1/2 (Cineriz/Italy) (1963)

Intensely autobiographical, Federico Fellini examines the creative process of a famous middle-aged Italian film director who is desperate to come up with some new inspiration as he's hounded not only by his professional colleagues but also by the press.

Guido Anselmi (Marcello Mastroianni) is suffering from "director's block." Stalled on his new science-fiction film, he escapes to a health resort to cure an undetermined illness. At the spa, he's forced to confront a series of personal as well as professional crises, precipitated by the complicated demands of Carla (Sandra Milo), his voluptuous mistress, and the inability of his wife Luisa (Anouk Aimee) to understand him. That leads to a confusion of childhood flashbacks, recurrent dreams, Catholic guilt and erotic fantasies.

After first considering Laurence Olivier, Fellini insisted that Mastroianni play his alterego and Claudia Cardinale embody the movie star Guido envisions as his Ideal Woman.

Utilizing a screenplay "La Bella Confusione" (a.k.a. "The Beautiful Confusion") co-written by Fellnini with Tullio Pinelli, Brunello Rondi and Ennio Flaiano, Fellini's innovative cinematic technique includes soaring aerial shots, jump cuts and zoom movements, enhanced by Gianni Di Venanzo's cinematography, Piero Gherardi's production/costume design and punctuated by Nino Rota's intoxicating music. Reportedly, Fellini attached a note to himself below the camera's eyepiece which read: "Ricordati che e un film comico" (a.k.a. "Remember, this is a comic film").

According to Fellini, the title is derived from the total of Fellini's previous six feature films (including "La Strada" and "La Dolce Vida") and three short films, making this his 8 ½ film. He's often confessed that his real-life Jungian psychoanalysis contributed to the bizarre, even grotesque imagery, and he chose black-and-white film because his dreams were always monochromatic. Like most Italian films at that time, the sound was entirely dubbed in afterward, allowing much of the dialogue to be written during post-production.

Nominated for five Academy Awards in 1963, it won for Best Foreign Language Film and Best Costume Design. Later, *8 ½* was the inspiration for Bob Fosse's *All That Jazz* and the Broadway musical *Nine*, which also became a movie.

On the Granger Movie Gauge of 1 to 10, *8 ½* is an enigmatic but brilliantly executed 8.5, delivering a playful, avant-garde insight into one of Italy's most celebrated filmmakers.

About Schmidt (New Line Cinema) (2002)

The glory of this character study is the magnificent Jack Nicholson. As sixty-six-year-old Warren Schmidt, a retired Omaha insurance company executive, he questions the significance of his life. He's irritated by his wife (June Squibb) of 42 years and has no desire to roam around the country in their 35-foot Winnebago. Watching television late one night, he impulsively signs up with Childreach as a foster parent. Then in a series of wildly inappropriate letters to Ndugu Umbo, an illiterate six-year-old Tanzanian boy, Schmidt pours his anger, frustration and remorse. Most of all, he's disappointed that his beloved and only daughter (Hope Davis) is about to marry Randall Hertzel (Dermot Mulroney), a dimwitted loser who sells waterbeds.

Hoping to change her mind, he drives to Denver, where he discovers more about what life really means than he ever imagined. What ensures our fixation on the screen is Jack, Jack, Jack. He seems totally liberated as an actor.

We seem to be gazing right into his soul as he delivers a ferociously riveting, Oscar-caliber performance. In a supporting role that includes a comic, nude hot-tub scene, Kathy Bates is amazing and pitch-perfect, as are the rest of the cast. Problem is: filmmakers Alexander Payne and Jim Taylor's (*Citizen Ruth*, "*Election*") bleak script, which depicts America's heartland as a contemporary bastion of tacky, beaten-down boredom, observing and commenting on the pathetic emptiness and alienation of those facing retirement age.

Ultimately, it's a depressing, existential soul-searching vision of a sad, lonely man who is desperate to discover a shred of purpose.

On the Granger Movie Gauge of 1 to 10, *About Schmidt* is a perceptive, satirical, yet profoundly affecting 9—and Jack Nicholson's performance is one of the season's must-sees.

The Adventures of Robin Hood
(Warner Bros.) (1938)

Filmed for $2 million in 1938, this action-packed adventure was the first widely successful live-action Technicolor movie, released a year before *The Wizard of Oz*.

When King Richard the Lion-Heart (Ian Hunter), who left England to fight in the Crusades, is taken captive, his wicked brother, Prince John (Claude Rains), with Sir Guy of Gisbourne (Basil Rathbone) and the Sheriff of Nottingham (Melville Cooper), plot to usurp the throne. Meanwhile, in Sherwood Forest, Sir Robin of Locksley (Errol Flynn) and his band of men vow to protect and provide for the Saxon poor by stealing from the Norman rich. So when Gisbourne and the Sheriff are escorting Richard's ward, Maid Marian (Olivia de Havilland), through the forest, they're kidnapped and held for ransom. They're soon released but not before Marian and Robin have fallen in love.

Scripted by Norman Reilley Raine and Seton I. Miller, inspired by Sir Walter Scott's novel *Ivanhoe* and DeKoven-Smith's opera *Robin Hood*, it was initially directed by Flynn's friend William Keighley, who was replaced by Michael Curtiz halfway through production. Originally, James Cagney was to play Robin with Anita Louise as Maid Marian, but after Cagney indignantly stalked off the lot, producer Hal B. Wallis took a chance on Tasmanian actor Flynn, who'd starred with de Havilland in *Captain Blood*.

According to Wallis' autobiography: "Errol was Robin to the life: good-humored, uninhibited, athletic...Whatever else he may have been, during Errol's nine years at Warner Bros., he was the golden cavalier of our studio. But his type of picture went out of fashion... the genre is dead, and there was only one Errol Flynn."

Belgian fencing master Fred Cevens and his son Albert taught the cast swordplay, while professional archer Howard Hill did all the trick shooting, including the arrow-splitting, when the contest was staged at Busch Gardens in Pasadena, CA. Well-padded stuntmen and bit players were paid $150 per shot for letting Hill hit them with arrows. Flynn did most of his own stunts except for a leap with his hands tied behind his back, another leap onto a horse, and his vault over Nottingham gate. Maid Marian's palomino horse was Golden Cloud – before he became known as Roy Rogers' Trigger.

On the Granger Movie Gauge of 1 to 10, *The Adventures of Robin Hood* is a swashbuckling 10, culminating in the most exciting swordfight ever filmed.

The Adventures of Tintin (Paramount Pictures) (2011)

After making his first Indiana Jones saga, Steven Spielberg heard many comparisons with a Belgian comic strip hero named Tintin, a plucky young reporter whose relentless pursuit of a good story catapults him into a world of high adventure. So now, in collaboration with Peter Jackson (*The Lord of the Rings*), Spielberg has fashioned a wondrous, breathtaking thrill-ride, utilizing Weta's state-of-the-art photorealistic, 3-D motion-capture animation.

One day in an outdoor flea market, wide-eyed Tintin (voiced by Jamie Bell), accompanied by his faithful white terrier Snowy, buys a scale model of an old warship ship called the Unicorn. As soon as he pays for his purchase, sinister Ivanovich Sakharine (voiced by Daniel Craig) tries to obtain it from him. But Tintin refuses. Then an American named Barnaby (voiced by Joe Starr) bids for it.

By now, Tintin's intrigued with his mysterious acquisition, curious as to the value it holds, as are the two incompetent (and identical) Interpol officers (voiced by British comedians Nick Frost and Simon Pegg). Then Tintin and his canine sidekick are kidnapped and tossed aboard the Karaboudjan, a steamer supposedly under the command of Capt. Archibald Haddock (voiced by Andy Serkis). But the salty, inebriated Captain is also being held hostage because he's a direct descendant of a 17th century naval commander who lost his ship, the Unicorn, to pirates led by evil Red Rackham (also voiced by Daniel Craig). Eventually, Tintin and Capt. Haddock join forces on a merry chase through the North African desert to the fictional Moroccan city of Bagghar, hoping to discover where a treasure trove is hidden.

Written by Steven Moffat (*Doctor Who*), Edgar Wright (*Shaun of the Dead*) and Joe Cornish (*Attack the Block*), based on a series of graphic books by Georges Remi, using the pseudonym Herge, and skillfully directed by Steven Spielberg, this exhilarating escapade is filled with relentlessly dashing derring-do and dastardly villainy.

On the Granger Movie Gauge of 1 to 10, *The Adventures of Tintin* is a terrific, fun-filled 10.

The African Queen (United Artists) (1951)

Although Humphrey Bogart won his only Oscar for playing Charlie Allnut, it's Katharine Hepburn's portrayal of straight-laced spinster Rosie Sayer that is primarily responsible for the enduring power of her iconic image.

In 1944, near the beginning of W.W.I, brother-and-sister Samuel (Robert Morley) and Rose (Hepburn) Sayer are Methodist missionaries in the village of Kungdu in East Africa. Their mail and supplies are delivered by slovenly Capt. Allnut (Bogart) on the steamer African Queen. When invading Germans kill Samuel and burn the village, Allnut offers to transport Rosie back to civilization. Although she abhors his drinking and gruff manner, and he loathes her pious, judgmental attitude, a friendship develops as they traverse treacherous waters and devise an ingenious way to destroy a German gunboat.

Securing financing for such an ambitious project was difficult, but Huston and producer Sam Spiegel raised money from London's Romulus Productions and Sound Services Inc, which supplied sound equipment to studios. Adapted by novelist/critic James Agee, John Collier, Peter Viertel and Huston, the script added a happy ending that didn't exist in British author C.S. Forester's 1935 novel.

Shot in a remote location in the Belgian Congo, this was a uniquely personal project for John Huston, who hunted elephant when he wasn't filming. That became the basis for Peter Viertel's novel *White Hunter, Black Heart*, directed by and starring Clint Eastwood.

Bogart, who hated Africa immediately, endured the application of real leeches for the scene where he tows the boat in chest-high water and reported that the infestation of ants was so severe in the cast/crew's makeshift bungalows that the legs of their beds were placed in pools of kerosene. Although bottled water was brought in, boiled and treated with halazone tablets, everyone got sick except Bogart and Huston, perhaps—as Huston observed—because they always drank water with scotch.

"While I was griping, Katie was in her glory," Bogart later told the press. "She couldn't pass by a fern or a berry without wanting to know its pedigree, and insisted on getting the Latin name for everything she saw walking, swimming, flying or crawling. She wallowed in that stinking hole!" Nominated for four 1951 Academy Awards, including Best Actor, Actress, Director and Screenplay, only Bogart won. While he'd previously denounced the Oscars as "silly" and "all bunk," when Greer Garson read his name, Bogart jogged onto the stage and cradled it as though it were a newborn baby.

On the Granger Movie Gauge of 1 to 10, *The African Queen* is an adventurous 10, a deeply touching, mature romance that's rich in pictorial beauty.

A.I.: Artificial Intelligence
(Warner Bros.) (2001)

Steven Spielberg is a cinematic genius. So was Stanley Kubrick. But this unconventional, collaborative effort may mystify movie-goers. Some will be beguiled, as I was. Others may be frustrated and/or disappointed. Told as a sci-fi fairy tale for adults, the story revolves around a perfect robotic child named David (Haley Joel Osment), adopted by a Cybertronics employee (Sam Robards) and his wife (Frances O'Connor) whose own seriously ill child (Jake Thomas) has been cryogenically frozen.

David is programmed to love, but those around him aren't— because he's 'mecha' (mechanical), not 'orga' (organic)—and, therein, lies his dilemma. Like Pinocchio, he yearns to be a real boy. But how? When he's abandoned with only his super toy Teddy bear as a companion, he's sets off in search of a dream.

Steeped in romanticism, the plot is divided into three segments: the domestic drama, the quest or odyssey, and then the futuristic underwater/ice sequences, a consequence of global warming. This fragmentation breeds problems. In the darkly disturbing road trip, for example, David meets up with Gigolo Joe (Jude Law), a 'love mecha,' who takes him to the Flesh Fair, a nightmarish carnival, filled with robot torture devices. Then the eerie, sentimental third segment evokes *E.T.* and *Close Encounters of a Third Kind*, moving grandly, yet tediously.

There's a lack of cohesion, a feeling of schizophrenia. Hayley Joel Osment is truly amazing and Jude Law is charismatic. The rich visuals—sets, costumes and creature/make-up effects—are stunning.

On the Granger Movie Gauge of 1 to 10, *A.I.: Artificial Intelligence* is an unpredictable, intriguing 10. Love it or hate it, it's a triumph of innovative film-making, a blend of science and humanity, and a brilliant collaboration of two acknowledged masters.

All the King's Men (Columbia Pictures) (1949)

In 2001, the United States Library of Congress selected this "culturally significant" 1949 socio-political drama for preservation in the National Film Registry, and it remains Oscar's last Best Picture winner to be based on a Pulitzer Prize-winning novel.

Jack Burden (John Ireland) is a newspaper reporter dispatched to rural Kanoma County to cover Willie Stark (Broderick Crawford), who is running for county treasurer and refusing to be intimidated by local politicians. A hick from the sticks, Stark's a populist who's been educated by his schoolteacher wife (Anne Seymour). After losing this first foray into politics, Stark studies law and becomes an idealistic attorney who fights for what is good. So when the Governor needs a weak flunky to run against him and split the vote of his rival, Stark is chosen. To everyone's surprise, Stark not only holds his own but wins with the help of Sadie (Mercedes McCambridge), his disillusioned, unscrupulous assistant/mistress. But nothing is quite what it seems when Burden delves beneath the layers of deceit and deception as philandering demagogue Stark becomes corrupted by his insatiable lust for power.

Produced, directed and adapted for the screen by Robert Rossen (*The Hustler*), the character study is loosely based on Robert Penn Warren's acclaimed novel about Louisiana's notorious 1930s Governor Huey *The Kingfish* Long.

When Rossen was cited by Sen. Joseph McCarthy's House Committee on Un-American Activities in 1947 for having Communist sympathies, my father, S. Sylvan Simon, who was then vice-president in charge of production at Columbia Pictures, came to his defense, convincing studio boss Harry Cohn to allow him to continue to develop this project, which was photographed by Burnett Guffey with newsreel intensity.

The Willy Stark role was originally offered to John Wayne, who turned it down, citing the script as unpatriotic, choosing to make *Sands of Iwo Jima* instead. And a very young John Derek is memorable as Stark's adopted son.

Nominated in six categories, it won three Academy Awards: Best Picture, Best Actor (Broderick Crawford) and Best Supporting Actress (Mercedes McCambridge). The inept 2006 remake, starring Sean Penn, Jude Law, Kate Winslet, James Gandolfini, Anthony Hopkins and Mark Ruffalo, pales in comparison.

On the Granger Movie Gauge of 1 to 10, the original version of *All the King's Men* is an iconic 10, a stunning screen adaptation of a literary classic.

Amelie (Miramax Zoe) (2001)

As France's official entry into the Foreign Film Oscar race, Jean-Pierre Jeunet's romantic comedy stars Audrey Tautou as Amelie, a shy, soft-spoken waitress at the Two Windmills cafe in Montmartre who puts her own love life on hold as she orchestrates the lives of those around her. Raised by her physician father after her mother was killed by a tourist plummeting off Notre Dame Cathedral, Amelie is a lonely, aloof young woman who uses her imagination as a prism to explore the world.

One day, behind a bathroom wall in her apartment, she discovers a small box of childhood toys that belong to the boy who lived there many years ago. Fascinated, she decides to return it to its rightful owner and, in watching his delight from afar, she gradually becomes bolder and out-going, concocting devious schemes to good deeds wherever she can – like altering the greengrocer's bad attitude, launching her father on a world tour, and match-making.

Pivotal to the change in her life is her love for Nino (Mathieu Kassovitz), a clerk in a sex shop who collects and reassembles tiny shreds of discarded photo machine snapshots. Director/writer Jeunet (*Delicatessen, City of Lost Children, Alien: Resurrection*) and co-writer Guillaume Laurant put a wry, fantastical, visually stylish spin on the old boy-meets-girl story, and the emotional delicacy of Audrey Tautou's exquisite Amelie could be compared with Audrey Hepburn's waifish Holly Golightly in *Breakfast at Tiffany's*, while director Mathieu Kassovitz (*Hate*) proves himself to be a sweetly offbeat, sexy actor.

On the Granger Movie Gauge of 1 to 10, *Amelie* is a frothy, funny, fanciful 10, a dazzling holiday confection. "Times are hard for dreamers," someone says, and perhaps that's what makes the *joie de vivre* of Amelie so timely.

An American in Paris (M.G.M.) (1951)

After producer Arthur Freed heard a concert of George Gershwin's tone poem *An American in Paris*, he casually mentioned to Ira Gershwin that he'd like to incorporate his late brother's orchestral composition as an integral part of a new picture Gene Kelly had proposed about an ex-GI, an aspiring painter who remains in Paris after the war. After negotiating for $158,750 to use the music, Gershwin agreed, arranging for an additional $56,250 to write any necessary new lyrics for other songs used. Thus was born one of the most imaginative M.G.M. musicals, directed by Vincente Minnelli from a charming Alan Jay Lerner script with John Alton's spectacular dance cinematography.

The love story, which is intercut with song-and-dance, revolves around artist Jerry Mulligan (Kelly) and his concert pianist friend, Adam Cook (Oscar Levant). Lonely, elegant socialite Milo Roberts (Nina Foch) is Jerry's benefactor, while he falls in love with Lise Bouvier (Leslie Caron), a French orphan he meets at a café. Problem is: Lise is already in a relationship with Henri Baurel (George Guetary), who sheltered her during W.W. II. The climax, an extravagant 17-minute ballet, evoking Jerry's fantasies as depicted by great French artists Renoir, Rousseau, Lautrec and Dufy, is rumored to have cost $450,000 to film.

Memorable musical numbers include "I've Got Rhythm," "Embraceable You," "Nice Work If You Can Get It," "S'Wonderful," "I'll Build a Stairway to Paradise" – a Follies-Bergere number with human candelabras, the delectable Viennese waltz parody "By Strauss" and "Our Love Is Here to Stay," the last song George Gershwin wrote before his death in 1937.

Originally, Maurice Chevalier and Yves Montand were considered for the part of Henri but both were eliminated for 'political' reasons and the part went to then-popular French performer Henri Baurel. And teenage Ballet des Champs-Elysees dancer Leslie Caron was cast only after Cyd Charisse discovered she was pregnant during pre-production.

On the Granger Movie Gauge of 1 to 10, *An American in Paris* is a tuneful 10, winning 1951 Academy Awards for Best Picture, Best Screenplay, Best Cinematography, Best Art/ Set Decoration, Best Costume Design, Best Musical Score, and Gene Kelly received an Honorary Oscar for "his versatility as an actor, singer, director, dancer and choreographer."

Argo (Warner Bros.) (2012)

Director/actor Ben Affleck adroitly combines the strength of a sensational, true-life story with relevant, politically-charged suspense that's strategically laced with humor—and the result is intense, exceptionally intelligent entertainment.

Set in 1979 and 1980 in Tehran, during the Iran hostage crisis, the plot revolves around six besieged American Embassy workers who seek refuge in the home of the Canadian Ambassador, Ken Taylor (Victor Garber). Knowing that if they're found by the militant Iranians, they'll be executed, along with the Ambassador and his wife, the Canadian and American governments, under the direction of then-President Jimmy Carter, turn to a CIA espionage advisor, Jack O'Donnell (Bryan Cranston), who calls in covert 'extraction' operative Tony Mendez (Affleck). His job is to rescue them—but how?

Realizing the worldwide appeal of the motion picture industry, Mendez inventively enlists the help of Hollywood makeup artist John Chambers (John Goodman), who, in turn, recruits flamboyant producer Lester Siegel (Alan Arkin), who blusters, "If I'm doing a fake movie, it's going to be a fake hit!"

Forming Studio Six Productions, they pretend to be scouting desert locations for an upcoming sci-fi adventure film, touted as "a cosmic conflagration." After forging their Canadian passports, Mendez then has to convince the terrified, bewildered hostages (Tate Donovan, Clea DuVall, Scoot McNairy, Rory Cochrane, Christopher Denham, Kerry Bishe) to assume their new aliases and 'show biz' identities as director, screenwriter, cinematographer, assistant producer, etc. —and conduct them out. But will capricious Iranian officials and suspicious Revolutionary Guards at the airport really believe their bizarre, far-fetched charade and allow them to escape?

Inspired by Joshuah Bearman's *Wired* magazine article, *The Great Escape*, and Antonio J. Mendez' book, *The Master of Disguise*, it's been scripted into a dandy, dramatic caper by Chris Terrio and skillfully directed by Ben Affleck (*The Town*, *Gone Baby Gone*) with meticulous attention to authentic historic detail, intercut with faux newsreel footage, to ensure credibility. Producer collaborators include George Clooney and Grant Heslov.

On the Granger Movie Gauge of 1 to 10, *Argo* is a compelling, high-tension 10—a terrific thriller!

The Artist (The Weinstein Company) (2011)

Imaginative, inventive and challenging, this almost totally silent film fantasy about the advent of talking pictures (1927-1931) was shot in Hollywood in black-and-white by a French crew headed by writer/director Michel Hazanavicius.

Genial George Valentin (Jean Dujardin) is a flamboyant matinee idol, reminiscent of Douglas Fairbanks. At the premiere of one of his movies at the Orpheum Theater, he accidentally encounters an ambitious, fun-loving flapper, Peppy Miller (Berenice Bejo), and is immediately intrigued by her. She gets her 'big break' and becomes a major star, while his allure is soon eclipsed by younger leading men who make the transition to 'talkies.'

Lining up for Oscar nominations, Jean Dujardin oozes the same kind of Gallic charm as Maurice Chevalier, while beautiful Berenice Bejo is sensational, evoking Marlene Dietrich, Joan Crawford and Gloria Swanson – who said it best in "Sunset Boulevard": "We didn't need dialogue. We had faces."

Plus, there are memorable performances by John Goodman, John Cromwell, Penelope Ann Miller and Uggy, the scene-stealing Boston terrier.

Film aficionados will recognize the familiar plot, combining the exuberant Gene Kelly/Debbie Reynolds romance from *Singin' in the Rain* with the poignant Norman Maine/Esther Blodgett premise of "A Star is Born." But Hazanavicius is neither nostalgic nor sentimental about the bygone era he's so faithfully recreated. Instead, he focuses a contemporary viewpoint on that kind of storytelling, acting, directing and visual style, capturing its dazzling spirit and elusive glamour—even filming at Mary Pickford's house.

Sharing in the credit for this extraordinary film are cinematographer Guillaume Schiffman, who sculpts with light and shadow, creating subtly impactful perspectives; composer Ludovic Bource, whose music conveys the mood of each scene; and production designer Laurence Bennett, making every detail not only accurate and authentic but perfect.

Winning Best Picture was a long shot, since only one silent movie, *Wings* (1927), has ever won the Oscar. But on the Granger Movie Gauge of 1 to 10, "The Artist" is an enchanting, exciting, visually eloquent 10. It's what classic cinema was all about...and definitely one of best films of 2011.

Australia (Twentieth Century Fox Corporation) (2008)

In one of the most ambitious, exciting filmmaking feats of the year, Baz Luhrmann has created a compelling, romantic frontier adventure that is, in its weight and grand ambition, on the epic scale of *Gone with the Wind*.

As viewed through the eyes of half-Aboriginal outcast child, Nullah (Brandon Walters), the story begins in 1939, when Lady Sarah Ashley (Nicole Kidman) travels from England to the inhospitable Australian outpost of Darwin to visit her husband's remote cattle station, Faraway Downs, only to discover that he's been killed by the scheming property manager (David Wenham) who's in cahoots with a ruthless cattle baron (Byran Brown).

Lady Sarah's only hope of saving the ramshackle Outback ranch lies with the Drover (Hugh Jackman), a feisty, restless stockman. Together - with the help of Nullah and his grandfather, King George (David Gulpilil), a mysterious Aboriginal shaman—they must drive 1500 head of cattle across the Kuraman Desert to market. Then in 1942, Japanese warplanes bomb Darwin with twice the airfreight they used to attack Pearl Harbor.

Stunningly successful both as a vibrant, emotional journey and as fascinating history, it's awesomely photographed, intensely emotional and creatively challenging, including an effective *Wizard of Oz* motif. Despite some raggedy editing, it goes over the top, then up and over again.

Nicole Kidman buries herself deep inside the character, conjuring up an incandescent image of a powerful, passionate woman shaped by destiny, Hugh Jackman's charismatic intensity holds you in thrall, and Brandon Walters is enchanting. Essential to any great melodrama are its villains: Bryan Brown is malevolent while David Wenham is loathsome.

On the Granger Movie Gauge of 1 to 10, *Australia* is an enormous, exotic, exhilarating 10. A must-see—this monumental movie stands way out from the crowd.

Avatar (20th Century-Fox) (2009)

Not since Dorothy's Kansas farmhouse landed in *The Wizard of Oz* – 70 years ago—and the screen transformed from black-and-white to color—has there been such a magical, revelatory moment, as the emergence of the planet Pandora in James Cameron's *Avatar* in IMAX 3-D. To call it a revolution in sci-fi imagery is an understatement.

In 2154, Earth has become dependent on a rare mineral, wryly named Unobtainium, mined by the Resources Development Administration on Pandora in the Alpha Centauri-A star system. To show a profit for RDA shareholders, chief administrator Carter Selfridge (Giovanni Ribisi) relies on Col.

Miles Quaritch (Stephen Lang) and his security force to maintain the safety and productivity of the human mining colony in the hostile atmosphere, while scientists under the leadership of botanist Grace Augustine (Sigourney Weaver) combine half-human, half-alien DNA in genetically-engineered avatars to develop a peaceful bridge-of-trust with the indigenous Na'vi, a deeply spiritual people.

To that end, a paraplegic former Marine, Jake Sully (Sam Worthington) is recruited to remotely control the avatar that matches his late twin brother's genome, and when Jake's avatar gets lost in the forest and is saved by the huntress Neytiri (Zoe Saldana), a Na'vi princess, and he forges a unique friendship with her clan. At the same time, he discovers that RDA forces are determined to strip mine the Na'vi's revered ancestral home/tribal habitat of 10,000 years, and a titanic battle ensues.

What's extraordinary is how Cameron and New Zealand's WETA Digital have created an exotic, paradisiacal, phosphorescent world. The lean, 10'-tall, blue-skinned Na'vi have huge yellow eyes and three-fingered hands and speak their own language.

Their ecologically-balanced, harmonious, bio-diverse environment encompasses a lush jungle and floating mountains, dominated by a gargantuan tree, along with wildlife like vicious viperwolves, six-legged direhorses, mighty thanators, gently graceful woodsprites, griffin-like banshees and the predatory leonopteryx. For 166 minutes, it's so dazzling that one can forgive simplistic storytelling, stereotypical characters and clunky dialogue.

On the Granger Movie Gauge of 1 to 10, *Avatar* is an exciting, spectacularly awesome 10. James Cameron is, once again, "king of the world."

Away from Her (Lionsgate) (2006)

What strength does the power of love have against the ravages of Alzheimer's? That's the question posed by twenty-eight-year-old actress-turned-writer/director Sarah Polley's powerful drama about the grace and the cruelty of aging.

Fiona (Julie Christie) and Grant (Gordon Pinsent) have been married for 44 years when he observes her placing a frying pan into the freezer after washing and drying it. Obviously, something's wrong.

As her mental capacity declines, Fiona becomes a danger to herself, wandering off and becoming lost. When it's obvious that he can no longer care for her, they agree that she should move into a nearby assisted-living facility. Soon Fiona becomes attached to another patient (Michael Murphy), as Grant relates to his pragmatic wife (Olympia Dukakis).

Independent, outspoken Sarah Polley tackles the screen adaptation of the Alice Munro short story *The Bear Came Over the Mountain*, saying: "I think the ways in which people are damaged are the ways in which they're strong," she says. "It's what makes people interesting—what they've overcome and how, and what they haven't and how that's become a good thing. Almost everyone's life is both a gorgeous story and a tragedy. I think being alive is really, really hard, and I'm constantly stunned and amazed by people who make it something interesting and wonderful."

Julie Christie remains as luminous as she was in *Darling* and *Dr. Zhivago*, and she's matched by Gordon Pinsent, a Canadian actor best known for "The Shipping News." Shot in the bitter cold of rural Ontario on a modest $4 million budget, it's one of the most mature movies to come along in a while.

On the Granger Movie Gauge of 1 to 10, *Away from Her* is an indelible, uncompromising 9, a sensitive testament to emotional endurance.

Battleship Potemkin
(1st Studio Goskino/USSR) (1925)

Produced in 1925 to commemorate the 1905 Revolution, *Battleship Potemkin* is a silent film directed by Sergei Mikahilovich Eisenstein as Marxist propaganda, presenting a dramatized version of the mutiny that occurred when the crew of the Russian battleship Potemkin rebelled against their Tsarist officers.

Set in the port town of Odessa, it's divided into five episodes: "Men and Maggots" in which the sailors refuse to eat *borsch* made with maggot-infested meat; "Drama on the Deck" in which the sailors mutiny and their Bolshevik leader, Vakulinchuk (Aleksandr Antonov), is killed; "A Dead Man Calls for Justice" in which Vakulinchuk's body is mourned by Odessa's populace; "The Odessa Staircase" in which marching Tsarist soldiers in their white summer tunics and mounted Cossacks brutally massacre helpless, innocent civilians; and "The Rendez-Vous with a Squadron" in which crews dispatched to intercept the Potemkin refuse to engage, lower their guns and join the Potemkin's sailors in solidarity.

Using primarily non-professional actors, Eisenstein filmed on location, using the marble steps leading down to the harbor and the battleship Twelve Apostles, sister ship of the original Potemkin which had been dismantled. Eisenstein formulated a modernist theory of editing, based on psychological perception.

Rhythm, motion, and repetition were three elements that distinguished his technique, along with concept of montage, a technique in which a series of short shots are edited into a sequence to condense space, time and information. At Goskino (the state film operation), Eisenstein trained as apprentice to newsreel cinematographer Eduard Tisse, who became his collaborator.

Battleship Potemkin premiered at the Moscow's Bolshoi Theater in December, 1925, but achieved its greatest success in 1926 in Berlin, Germany, where it riveted artists ranging from Fritz Lang to Bertolt Brecht and theater directors Edwin Piscator and Max Reinhardt. Irish-born painter Francis Bacon's work was profoundly affected, and Charlie Chaplin cited it as his favorite movie. When Brian De Palma was filming *The Untouchables* (1987) and needed a sequence of random terror and violence, he lifted the famous baby carriage-bumping-down-the-steps scene, almost intact, and used it.

On the Granger Movie Gauge of 1 to 10, *Battleship Potemkin* is an influential 10. Named the greatest film of all time at the 1958 Brussels World's Fair, it has been restored and released, accompanied by a new arrangement of Edmund Meisel's orchestral score.

Beasts of the Southern Wild (Fox Searchlight Pictures) (2012)

A film festival favorite from Sundance to Cannes, this unlikely story merges "the poetics of an art film with something that feels like 'Die Hard,'" according to its twenty-nine-year-old director Benh Zeitlin.

Set in a post-Hurricane Katrina Louisiana swampland, the relationship story revolves around an unruly, precocious six-year-old African-American girl called Hushpuppy (Quvenzhane Wallis), who lives in a ramshackle hut connected by a long rope to the treehouse shack inhabited by her ailing, alcoholic father, Wink (Dwight Henry). Apparently, her mother "swam away" years earlier.

Acutely aware of the concrete levee that separates dry land from their tidal basin, called the Bathtub, Hushpuppy imagines the coming flood in terms of Arctic avalanches, releasing fantastic, prehistoric, boar-like creatures called aurochs. Even when a ferocious storm destroys her environment, she's a relentlessly optimistic survivalist, firmly believing that balance is the natural order of the universe.

Evoking *The Adventures of Huckleberry Finn*, the narrative is presented in Hushpuppy's poetic voiceover, illuminating with magical realism her wonderment about the brutal, primordial wilderness in which she lives—particularly when she's on a raft fashioned from an empty truck bed.

After meeting as teens at New York's Young Playwrights' festival, writer/musician/director Benh Zeitlin and Florida Panhandle native Lucy Alibar developed their concept, based on Alibar's off-off Broadway play *Juicy and Delicious*. Originally, the main character was a nine-year-old boy but when charismatic Quvenzhane Wallis appeared at an open audition, the part was altered to suit her. Other roles are also played by non-actors, like New Orleans baker Dwight Henry. Their grizzled faces with missing teeth resonate with authenticity.

A study of why people go to the movies concluded that we want to cross the transom of our social universe and enter the lives of people we cannot know in our own neighborhood. That's what this movie accomplishes, delivering not only knowledge but ideas, which is why it's significant.

On the Granger Movie Gauge of 1 to 10, *Beasts of the Southern Wild* is a thrilling, transfixing 10, an evocative, contemporary allegory.

Being John Malkovich (USA Films) (1999)

If there's an award for the boldest, most unconventional and wildly inventive movie of the year, it has to go to *Being John Malkovich*, in which screenwriter Charlie Kaufman and director Spike Jonze blend surrealism with science-fiction and self-parody. John Cusack stars as an out-of-work puppeteer who takes a job as a filing clerk in a New York office building on the 7 1/2 floor, where the rents are low because the ceilings are half the normal height. It's a great visual gag as workers hunch over, scuttling down the hall. Stuck in an unhappy marriage to an almost unrecognizable Cameron Diaz with dark, frizzy hair, he becomes infatuated with a co-worker, Catherine Keener, who couldn't be less interested. At least until he discovers a small door behind a filing cabinet that leads to a tunnel which, inexplicably, sucks him into the brain of actor John Malkovich.

Cusack can see through the actor's eyes and share whatever he's is feeling—for 15 minutes—until he's dumped into a ditch on the New Jersey Turnpike.

When he shares his discovery with Keener, she immediately sees the potential in selling entrance—$200 per person—to this portal so that others can partake in the sensory and emotional experiences of John Malkovich. They become partners in this commercial venture—until, inevitably, the enigmatic

Malkovich discovers how they've opened this "metaphysical can of worms." Plus, there's a deliriously mad subplot of gender/blender sexual seduction, absurdist supporting gems from Orson Bean and Mary Kay Place, plus witty cameos by Charlie Sheen, Sean Penn, and Brad Pitt.

On the Granger Movie Gauge of 1 to 10, *Being John Malkovich* is a clever, outrageous 10. It's a film of astonishing and beguiling originality.

The Best Exotic Marigold Hotel (Fox Searchlight Pictures) (2011)

Culture shock lies in store for seven, cash-strapped senior Brits who board a plane from London to Jaipur, ready to embark on the third act of their lives.

There's recently widowed Evelyn Greenslade (Judi Dench), retired High-Court Judge Graham Dashwood (Tom Wilkinson), lonely Madge Hardcastle (Celia Imrie), randy Norman Cousins (Ronald Pickup), quarrelsome Douglas and Jean Ainslie (Bill Nighy, Penelope Wilton), and former housekeeper Muriel Donnelly (Maggie Smith) who, while awaiting a low-cost hip replacement, adamantly refuses to eat anything she doesn't know how to pronounce.

Their destination in India is the once stately but now dilapidated hotel which is managed as a retirement residence "for the elderly and beautiful" by relentlessly optimistic, if hopelessly inexperienced Sonny Kapoor (Dev Patel from *Slumdog Millionaire*). Enthusiastic Sonny's sincere earnestness tries to compensate for the lack of doors, functional telephones and plumbing as he pursues the 'forbidden' love of his life, Sunaina (Indian actress Tena Desai), a call center worker.

Adapted from the 2004 novel *These Foolish Things* by Deborah Moggach, this bittersweet, fish-out-of-water comedic drama, poignantly scripted by Ol Parker and compassionately directed by John Madden (*Shakespeare in Love, The Debt*), is a bit reminiscent of Robert Altman's interweaving ensembles, along with *Enchanted April* and *Cocoon*, in the way the lives of these expectant travelers are radically changed as they encounter challenges in this foreign culture and accommodate to its customs.

On a deeper level, there's a subtle, heartfelt commentary on 'outsourcing' the elderly, along with customer service call centers, in countries where their limited funds will go further.

The accomplished cast of seasoned thespians makes the most out of every witty scene, along with a character unto itself: the distinctively architected hotel, a former chieftain's palace, located several hundred miles southwest of Udaipur. Cinematographer Ben Davis artfully captures the inherent cacophony and incessant chaos of careening tuk-tuks in the vividly colorful street scenes.

On the Granger Movie Gauge of 1 to 10, *The Best Exotic Marigold Hotel* is an adventurous 8. Anglophiles should check in and check it out.

A Better Life (Summit Entertainment) (2011)

Oscar season is many months away but, hopefully, nominators and voters will remember Mexican actor Demian Bichir because he delivers a powerhouse performance in this poignant father/son drama, set in East Los Angeles.

Carlos Galindo (Demian Bichir) is a hard-working single father. He's an illegal Mexican immigrant but his sullen fourteen-year-old son Luis (Jose Julien) was born in the United States and is, therefore, entitled to citizenship. Although he earns barely a subsistence salary as part of a landscaping crew, when Carlos's boss offers to sell him his battered old truck, it seems like a key to the door of opportunity.

"You're not just buying a truck," his buddy says. "You're buying the American Dream."

Being undocumented, Carlos cannot get a driver's license so he's not only law-abiding but extra careful because the fear of arrest and deportation hovers over everyone in his Hispanic community. But when a day laborer steals the treasured truck when he's trimming the fronds on a tall palm tree, Carlos has no choice but to set off in pursuit. With Luis at his side, they struggle overcome the myriad of obstacles thrown in their path and learn far more about each other in their quest to retrieve what is rightfully theirs.

Written by Eric Eason (*Manito*) from a story by Roger L. Simon, it's sensitively directed by Chris Weitz (*Twiight: New Moon, The Golden Compass, About a Boy, American Pie*), whose grandmother, Mexican actress Lupita Tovar, emigrated in the 1920s and whose wife is half-Cuban/half-Mexican.

Earnestly sincere and, perhaps, sentimental, it's nevertheless captivating, reminiscent of Vittorio De Sica's 1948 neo-realistic Italian classic, "The Bicycle Thief." Spanish cinematographer Javier Aguirresarobe captures glimpses of Los Angeles that are rarely photographed, including an authentic "charro" or Mexican rodeo, accented by an Alexandre Desplat's Latin-inflected musical score.

And if Demian Bichir looks familiar: he's played the scary drug kingpin Esteban on Showtime's *Weeds* and Castro in *Che*.

On the Granger Movie Gauge of 1 to 10, *A Better Life* is a timely, compassionate 8, illuminating the contemporary immigrant experience.

Big Fish (Columbia Pictures) (2003)

This is the multi-layered history of charming, irascible Edward Bloom (Albert Finney), a consummate story-teller who weaves the improbable events of his life in Ashton, Alabama, into an elaborate tapestry of tall-tales.

As he lies dying, his wife (Jessica Lange) summons home their estranged son (Billy Crudup), a reporter based in Paris, who begs for the truth, asking, "Who are you?" So, in flashbacks, the wild, weird adventures of his father's life unfold.

Years ago, young Edward (Ewan McGregor), "a man intended for larger things," embarked on an odyssey which began with a gentle giant (Matthew McGrory) and stumbling into the idyllic town of Specter. Subsequently, he befriended some quirky, colorful characters, including a circus ring-master (Danny DeVito), a rueful bank robber (Steve Buscemi), and conjoined twins (Ada & Arlene Tai). Then there's the fanciful courtship of his wife (Alison Lohman) at Auburn. But most influential was the enchanted witch (Helena Bonham Carter) who told him that "the biggest fish in the river gets that way by never being caught," a philosophy he quickly embraced.

Adapted by John August from Daniel Wallace's *Big Fish: A Novel of Mythic Proportions*, this innovative, inventive fable of paternal conflict revolves around the surreal visual brilliance of director Tim Burton, augmented by Philippe Rousselot's awesome cinematography and Danny Elfman's musical score. Does magical realism always make sense? No. But Albert Finney, Tim Burton and all the creators of "Big Fish" should be contenders for Oscar gold.

On the Granger Movie Gauge of 1 to 10, *Big Fish* is a wondrous, magical 10. Reality is highly over-rated. Go for fantasy. Catch one of the best films of the year!

Billy Elliot (Universal Focus) (2000)

Beginning with an exuberant title sequence, this charming, off-beat, coming-of-age story revolves around Billy Elliot, the younger of two sons of a widower coal miner in Northern England. It's 1984, and the miners are engaged in a long, bitter strike. Following the family tradition, Billy is expected to learn boxing at the Everington Boys Club where, instead, the eleven-year-old becomes enthralled by the girls' dancing class, led by a chain-smoking teacher who recognizes his raw talent. But when his macho father and rabble-rousing brother discover he's taking ballet lessons, they ridicule Billy ("Lads do boxing and football and wrestling, not friggin' ballet."), forcing him to hide his slippers under the mattress and sneak off to class. Then come the auditions for the Royal Ballet School and Billy's joyful, foot-stompin' "I Want to Boogie" sequence.

What makes this heartfelt English import such a gem is the collaboration of writer Lee Hall, cinematographer Brian Tufano and director Stephen Daldry, who—despite the simplistic predictability of the plot—create eccentric, lovable characters and evocative imagery.

As Billy, Jamie Bell embodies awkward determination, juggling grim reality with a surreal fantasy world. ("Just because I like ballet doesn't mean I'm a pouf!") As his father, Gary Lewis is tough-yet-tender, and Julie Walters scores as Billy's crusty yet compassionate teacher. Jamie Draven and Stuart Wells lend strong support with Jean Heywood touching as Billy's senile grandmother who recalls, "I could have been a professional dancer." While the bleak setting is reminiscent of *The Full Monty*, the energetic mood evokes *Flashdance*.

On the Granger Movie Gauge of 1 to 10, *Billy Elliot* is an exhilarating 8. Combining comedy and poignancy, it's all about being yourself.

Born Yesterday (Columbia Pictures – original 1950 version)

Judy Holliday became Hollywood's definitive dumb, brassy blonde, winning a Golden Globe and an Academy Award as Best Actress for playing Billie Dawn, a role she originated on Broadway.

The plot revolves around junk tycoon Harry Brock (Broderick Crawford) and his girl-friend Billie Dawn (Holliday) who arrive in Washington, D.C. so Harry can buy some influence in Congress. Realizing Billie's intellectual limitations, he hires political reporter Paul Verrall (William Holden) to educate her so she won't embarrass him. But opening Billie's mind is a revelation, as she acquires knowledge and begins to understand what America stands for and how dishonest Harry really is.

Columbia Pictures was the first film studio ever to pay $1 million for a literary property. At the time, my father, S. Sylvan Simon, was vice-president in charge of production under notorious tycoon Harry Cohn, whom—years later—playwright Garson Kanin acknowledged was the model for Harry Brock.

Although Cohn initially questioned whether comedienne Judy Holliday could make the transition from stage to screen, Broderick Crawford, who had just won an Oscar as a crooked politician in *All the King's Men*, was cast as Harry Brock, replacing cantankerous Paul Douglas, and William Holden became Paul Verrall with the understanding that screenwriter Albert Mannheimer, who revised Garson Kanin's play, garnering a Writer's Guild Award and Oscar nomination, would build up the journalist's role.

Director George Cukor rehearsed the actors for two weeks and had them perform in front of an audience of studio employees before location shooting began in Washington, D.C. As directed by Cukor, Billie and Harry's long, silent game of gin-rummy is one of the screen's comedic highlights. On the four-day train trip to Washington, Judy Holliday and Broderick Crawford reportedly played gin every day – with Holliday winning $600 en route. While Cukor was nominated as Best Director and the film as Best Picture, only Holliday brought home the coveted Oscar.

Born Yesterday was revived on Broadway in 1989 with Madeline Kahn, Ed Asner and Daniel Hugh Kelly, and a disappointing film sequel was made in 1993 with Melanie Griffith, John Goodman and Don Johnson.

On the Granger Movie Gauge of 1 to 10, the original *Born Yesterday* is an iconic 10. As Verrall puts it, "A world full of ignorant people is too dangerous to live in."

Bridge of Spies (DreamWorks/Disney/Fox) (2015)

Master filmmaker Steven Spielberg is fascinated with exploring history: *Schindler's List, Saving Private Ryan, Munich, Amistad,* and *Lincoln.* Now, *Bridge of Spies* ...

In New York City in the 1950s, at the height of the simmering Cold War between the United States and the Soviet Union, painter Rudolf Abel (Mark Rylance) is captured and accused of being a Russian spy. Summoned by his boss (Alan Alda), insurance lawyer James B. Donovan (Tom Hanks) is told to represent Abel. A former prosecutor at the Nuremburg trials, Donovan's known as a wily, pragmatic mediator.

Reluctant at first, Donovan is, nevertheless, determined to defend his client, insisting on "due process of law," even when the presiding judge and the American public have deemed Abel guilty, and Donovan's wife (Amy Ryan) and family are harassed in their Brooklyn home.

Sometime later, U.S. Air Force pilot Francis Gary Powers (Austin Stowell) is shot down over Soviet airspace. Both men possess sensitive information, becoming pawns, traded by their respective nations.

So CIA director Allen Dulles (Peter McRobbie) directs Donovan to fly to Berlin to broker the covert, danger-fraught deal, which is further complicated by the arrest of a young American student, Frederic Pryor (Will Rogers), detained in the Eastern sector behind the newly-erected Wall.

Co-scripted by Ethan & Joel Coen with Matt Charman, based on Donovan's *Strangers on a Bridge: The Case of Colonel Abel and Francis Gary Powers* (1964), Spielberg creates an intensely suspenseful saga, culminating on the Glienicki Bridge over the Havel River.

As usual, Spielberg surrounds himself with the most talented actors and crew. Tom Hanks is flawless as a steadfast, idealistic, yet canny negotiator with a dry sense of humor, while Mark Rylance impresses with commanding finesse and ironic discretion. Cinematographer Janusz Kaminski dazzles with a sequence of Powers ejecting from his U-2 surveillance plane, viewing its destruction through his parachute. Augmenting the dark subterfuge are Adam Stockhausen's production design and Thomas Newman's score.

On the Granger Movie Gauge of 1 to 10, *Bridge of Spies* is an enthralling 10, an espionage thriller with contemporary relevance.

Brooklyn (Fox Searchlight Pictures) (2015)

The emotionally tempestuous, Irish immigrant experience serves as the basis for this sweetly poignant, assimilation story.

In 1952, the local Roman Catholic Church arranges for demure, 20'ish Eilis Lacey (Saoirse Ronan) to reluctantly leave her widowed mother (Jane Brennan) and older sister Rose (Fiona Glascott) in Enniscorthy, County Wexford, to live and work in Brooklyn, New York.

Naïve and bewildered after her long ocean voyage, she arrives at a small boarding-house that's strictly run by stern, sharp-tongued Mrs. Kehoe (Julie Walters) and begins a job at a local department store, where her shy, prim demeanor doesn't exactly encourage customers.

Wretchedly lonely and homesick, Eilis is sponsored by a warmly sympathetic priest (Jim Broadbent), who suggests that she take night courses in accounting and attend Church dances. That's where she meets Tony (Emory Cohen), an impetuous Italian-American plumber who has a penchant for Irish girls.

When Tony invites Eilis home to meet his family, the boardinghouse girls insist on giving her lessons on how to properly eat spaghetti – and the results are hilarious.

Then, just as Eilis makes a romantic commitment to Tony, tragedy strikes and she's summarily summoned back home, where she's ardently pursued by Jim Farrell (Domhnall Glee-son), a highly eligible suitor.

So Eilis is faced with a dilemma: should she remain in southern Ireland, where she's comfortable, or return to Brooklyn to forge a new life for herself?

Director John Crowley (*Boy A, Intermission*), working from a script by Nick Hornby (*About a Boy, An Education*), based on Colm Toibin's popular novel, has created a classic, sensitive love story, propelled by Saoirse Ronan, using her natural Irish accent to deliver low-key, yet powerful, Awards-caliber performance.

And Crowley's production crew adds to the luster – including cinematographer Yves Belanger, designer Francois Seguin, set decorator Suzanne Cloutier, costumer Odile Ficks-Mireaux, and composer Michael Brook.

On the Granger Movie Gauge of 1 to 10, *Brooklyn* is an escapist 8, enhanced by a superbly confident ensemble.

The Bucket List (Warner Bros.) (2007)

I t's time to rejoice—the darkly comic *The Bucket List* is a gift for moviegoers.

Crusty, cranky corporate billionaire Edward Cole (Jack Nicholson) and knowledgeable garage mechanic Carter Chambers (Morgan Freeman) become unlikely friends as they share a hospital room. Terminally ill with cancer yet feeling fine, they both realize they have 'unfinished business.'

In an exercise in forward thinking, they make a list of everything they want to do before they "kick the bucket" and embark on the most unlikely road trip you can imagine: skydiving, race car driving and laughing 'till they cry. While they relish their high-flying adventures – exploring Egypt's pyramids, a safari in Tanzania, the Taj Mahal and the Great Wall of China—they also learn more about themselves and what really matters on this often-confusing journey of life.

Charming Jack Nicholson's sly, twisted nature has an irresistible appeal. As an actor, he is totally liberated, creating one of the most memorable characters this year, while Morgan Freeman is extraordinary, completely believable, delivering a quietly composed and curiously touching performance. Together, they get away with outrageous gallows humor and black comedy that would sink more timid thespians. Their tandem performances are near to perfection.

Evoking memories of *The Odd Couple* and *Grumpy Old Men*, screenwriter Justin Zackham's dialogue is deft, intelligent and laced with an outrageous sense of humor, while veteran director Rob Reiner understands the frailty and absurdity of the human condition.

While there are editing and continuity glitches, particularly the CGI superimposing the actors' faces during the stunt work, they barely detract from the characters' emotional wallop.

On the Granger Movie Gauge of 1 to 10, *The Bucket List* is a 9— a heartfelt, wickedly funny, one-of-a-kind treat.

Cape Fear (Universal International) (1962)

This 1962 psychological horror thriller catapulted insouciant actor Robert Mitchum into cinema history books as one of the screen's scariest, most sadistic psychopaths. Dapperly clad in a white Panama hat and suit, he's devilishly tall, dark and clever.

When Max Cady (Mitchum) is released after spending many years in prison for rape, he's determined to torment and wreak revenge on prosecuting attorney Sam Bowden (Gregory Peck), who lives with his wife Peggy (Polly Bergen) and young daughter Nancy (Lori Martin) in a small Southern town. First, Cady poisons their dog. Then he menaces Nancy and whispers obscenities to Peggy over the telephone.

But, even when he brutally abuses bar girl Diane Taylor (Barrie Chase), neither Police Chief Mark Dutton (Martin Balsam) nor private detective Charlie Sievers (Telly Savalas) can prove smirking Cady's guilt for any of these crimes. Desperate, Sam hires some thugs to beat Cady; instead, under a boardwalk, Cady wipes out his attackers and continues to terrorize the Bowdens. At this point, Sam hustles his family onto their houseboat in the swamplands of Cape Fear – with Cady following close behind.

Adapted by James R. Webb from the novel *The Executioners* by John D. MacDonald, it's tautly directed by J. Lee Thompson (*The Guns of Navarone*). Gregory Peck, who bought the rights to MacDonald's book, wanted to play opposite Robert Mitchum, who had established his villainous credentials as the homicidal preacher in *The Night of the Hunter* (1955), so he delivered a case of bourbon to Mitchum's home.

"OK, I've drunk your bourbon and I'm drunk," he subsequently told Peck. "I'll do it." Peck and Thompson had also wanted Hayley Mills to play the daughter but Walt Disney would not release her from exclusive contract.

The scene in which Robert Mitchum attacks Polly Bergen on the houseboat was almost completely improvised. When J. Lee Thompson slipped Mitchum raw eggs to smear on Bergen, she was stunned and her reaction was real. Bergen then got battered and bruised when he dragged her through various doors, which a crew member had inadvertently left locked, so the hapless actress was, literally, used as a battering ram.

On the Granger Movie Gauge of 1 to 10, *Cape Fear* is a claustrophobic, diabolically gripping 10—and far better than the 1991 remake, starring Robert De Niro, in which director Martin Scorsese featured Mitchum, Peck and Balsam in cameos.

Casablanca (Warner Bros.) (1942)

When filming began in 1942, this suspenseful, bittersweet melodrama was called *Everybody Comes to Rick's*, focusing on a man and a woman who were willing to sacrifice their love for each other—because it was the right thing to do.

As W.W. II spreads across Europe, thousands of refugees are seeking asylum in Casablanca, using political connections or personal influence to obtain exit visas or, better yet, letters to transit to fly to Lisbon, Portugal, en route to America. Ruthless Gestapo officer, Major Heinrich Strasser (Conrad Veidt) and Captain Renault (Claude Rains), the prefect of police, are watching Victor Lazlo (Paul Henreid), an influential Czechoslovakian resistance leader, and his gentle wife, Ilsa Lund (Ingrid Bergman), as they visit Rick's Cafe Americane, hoping to obtain those precious papers.

Years earlier, Ilsa had a romance in Paris with its mysteriously apolitical proprietor, Rick Blaine (Humphrey Bogart), at a time when she thought Lazlo was dead—and that's acknowledged by Rick's piano-player, Sam (hoarse-voiced Dooley Wilson), with their theme song, *As Time Goes By*.

Curiously, neither Bogart nor Bergman was originally cast. Instead, Ronald Reagan was to play Rick with Ann Sheridan, Michele Morgan or Hedy Lamarr as Isla. But all that changed when studio exec Hal Wallis decided to transform a stalwart supporting actor named Humphrey Bogart into a romantic leading man and borrow luminous Ingrid Bergman, a Swedish actress who was under contract to David O. Selznick.

Written by brothers Julius and Phillip Epstein and Howard Koch (additional material by Casey Robinson), it's directed by versatile Michael Curtiz (*The Adventures of Robin Hood, Mildred Pierce, Life with Father*) and photographed by Arthur Edeson. And contrary to recollections of some of the performers, there was never any question that the heroine would ultimately leave Casablanca with her husband.

Extraordinarily timely, the premiere was held only 19 days after the Allies landed in North Africa, and the film was playing in theaters when Roosevelt and Churchill chose Casablanca as their next meeting site.

On the Granger Movie Gauge of 1 to 10, *Casablanca* is a tension-filled 10, filled with romantic intrigue.

Cast Away (20th Century-Fox/ DreamWorks) (2000)

Along with a sure-fire Oscar nomination, Tom Hanks gets my vote for this year's REAL *Survivor*. In this contemporary Robinson Crusoe tale, Hanks plays a busy FedEx executive who waves good-bye to his girlfriend, Helen Hunt, saying "I'll be right back." They've just exchanged Christmas gifts. She gave him her grandfather's pocket watch with her photo inside and he gave her a little, square jeweler's box, presumably an engagement ring.

Then there's the harrowing agony of a terrifying plane crash, and Hanks washes ashore on a tiny, deserted speck of an island in the Pacific Ocean. How will he find water, food and shelter with nothing but the clothes he's wearing, a scavenged flashlight and the contents of FedEx boxes strewn on the beach?

Using ingenuity, he turns ice-skate blades into knives, videotape into rope, dress material into a fishing net and triumphantly builds a fire. With his own blood, he paints a face on a volleyball and it becomes his companion named Wilson. But even more important than his grueling physical and mental endurance is his metaphysical meditation in the solitary silence and his eventual transformation from a selfish, time-obsessed workaholic into a thoughtful, mature man, fully capable, four years later, of coping with a challenging crossroad of choices.

Actor/producer Tom Hanks and director Robert Zemeckis, who collaborated on another Everyman journey called *Forrest Gump*, superbly craft this risky, often humorous film and, along with writer William Broyles Jr., they are as distinguished for the paths not chosen, the pitfalls avoided.

On the Granger Movie Gauge of 1 to 10, *Cast Away* is an intense, ironic,insightful 10— one of the 10 Best Pictures of the Year. It's not just a movie—it's an experience.

Catch Me If You Can (Dream Works) (2002)

O nce again, truth is stranger than fiction, and this enthralling cat-and-mouse game was inspired by the exploits of audacious Frank W. Abagnale Jr., known as the Skywayman. From the time he ran away from his troubled home at age 16 to his capture at 21, Abagnale passed himself off as a co-pilot on Pan Am, an Emergency Room physician, a lawyer and a millionaire. He was so skilled at 'paperhanging' (check fraud) — and had such chutzpah—that, for years, he was able to outwit and outmaneuver FBI Agent Carl Hanratty, who patiently pursued him around the world while developing a curious surrogate-father/son relationship with the daring identity thief.

While Leonardo DiCaprio is engaging as the self-assured, elusive master of deception, it's Tom Hanks' dogged determination as the stodgy agent that resonates, along with Christopher Walken's poignant portrayal of Abagnale's father, a glib, small-town jeweler in trouble with the IRS while desperately clinging to his adulterous French war-bride (Nathalie Baye). Perceptively directed by Steven Spielberg from Jeff Nathanson's expertly-plotted screenplay, based on Abagnale's memoir, it's a cockeyed version of the American dream: an ingenious, jet-setting grifter who scammed bad checks in 50 states and 26 countries, bilking banks of $2.5 million, yet who's still haunted by the sins of his parents which fractured his family.

After serving five years, Abagnale was released from prison on the condition that he teach law enforcement to prevent fraud. Now he has his own security firm and lectures at the FBI Academy.

On the Granger Movie Gauge of 1 to 10, *Catch Me If You Can* is an amazing, astonishing 10. For sheer escapist entertainment, this rebellious rogue's skewed survival game is a winner. It's one of my top ten BEST MOVIES of 2002.

Charlotte's Web (Paramount Pictures) (2006)

In E.B. White's novel, a tiny pig discovers that the most precious gift in the world is the bond of friendship. Now this beloved, quintessentially American children's tale—which was previously made into a 1973 Hanna-Barbera cartoon—is on the screen in live-action, combining barnyard animals with *Babe*-like CG-assisted animatronics.

Set in New England, the fantasy begins when strong-willed, young Fern Arable (Dakota Fanning) realizes that her father (Kevin Anderson) is going to dispose of a runt-of-the-litter spring piglet. Determined to save his life, she rescues him, naming him Wilbur. When Wilbur (voice of Dominic Scott Kay) grows too big to be a house pet, he's placed across the street in farmer Zuckerman's barn where he's befriended by Charlotte (maternal-sounding Julia Roberts), a very wise and gracious spider who lives high up in the rafters.

Her devotion to naive Wilbur is boundless and, with the reluctant help of the selfish rat Templeton (voice of Steve Buscemi), she devises an ingenious way to try to save him from a porker's inevitable fate in the smokehouse – much to the amazement of their comical barn-yard companions (voices of John Cleese, Cedric the Entertainer, Oprah Winfrey, Kathy Bates, Reba McEntire and Robert Redford).

In addition to E.B. White's whimsical characters, writers Susannah Grant and Kery Kirk-patrick, along with director Gary Winick (*13 Going on 30*) have added two dimwitted crows (voices of Thomas Hayden Church and Andre Benjamin), a rotten goose egg and the inevi-table flatulence jokes.

Visually, the film is glorious—and it all works, capturing not only every subtle nuance but the transcendent essence of E.B. White cycle-of-life theme.

On the Granger Movie Gauge of 1 to 10, *Charlotte's Web* weaves a magical 10, becoming the best family film of the year.

Chicago (Miramax) (2002)

There's more razzle-dazzle in *Chicago* than I've seen in years. Directed by Rob Marshall and adapted by screenwriter Bob Condon from the hit Broadway show by John Kander/Fred Ebb/Bob Fosse, this hip musical sparkles and sizzles, opening with sultry Catherine Zeta-Jones strutting *All That Jazz*. Can she sing? You bet. So can Renee Zellweger and Richard Gere.

Set in the 1929 moral meltdown of the Windy City, this cynical story revolves around two murderesses, Velma Kelly (Zeta-Jones) and Roxie Hart (Zellweger), in Cook County jail awaiting trial. Velma's a big vaudeville star while Roxie's a goofy, dreamy, ambitious wannabe. They loathe each other as they compete for the attention of their slick, shrewd lawyer, Billy Flynn (Gere).

As Roxie's hapless husband (John C. Reilly) hovers in the background, their rivalry is encouraged by the conniving prison matron (Queen Latifah). But what was straightforward on the stage becomes a surreal kaleidoscope of reality and fantasy as Roxie's imagination blends the sleazy spotlight of notoriety with celebrity—not unlike contemporary headline-hogging murder trials.

By using that innovative device, Rob Marshall is able to transcend the limits of the stage production, deepen its emotional power and clarify its intention. There's an ingenious number in which Zellweger sits on Gere's lap, like a ventriloquist's dummy, while he talks to the press. Then Gere gingerly tap-dances as he cleverly bamboozles the jury. Even Chita Rivera from the original cast does a cameo.

On the Granger Movie Gauge of 1 to 10, *Chicago* is a spectacular, thrilling 10, winning Oscar gold. Rarely has a Broadway show been transferred to the screen as inventively and successfully.

Chitty Chitty Bang Bang (D.F.I. Picture) (1968)

Best known as the creator of James Bond, British writer Ian Fleming also dreamed up this children's fantasy about an eccentric inventor who uses his magical flying car to rescue children. Set in the early 20th century, the story opens with a Grand Prix race in which one of the cars swerves to avoid a dog and crashes. Widower Caractacus Potts (Dick Van Dyke) rebuilds it – to the delight of his two children, Jeremy (Adrian Hall) and Jemima (Heather Ripley), and a beautiful upper-class lady, Truly Scrumptious (Sally Ann Howes), who joins them for a picnic at the beach and other fanciful adventures, including eluding the scary, villainous Child Catcher (Robert Helpmann).

Scripted by Roald Dahl (*Charlie and the Chocolate Factory, James and the Giant Peach*), it's directed by Ken Hughes, who helmed the Bond adventure "You Only Live Twice," and produced by Albert "Cubby" Broccoli, who produced all the Bond films. The car itself was based on three different racecars owned by Polish auto enthusiast Count Louis Zboroswki. As the story goes, Broccoli's wife found one of Zboroswki's original cars at a London auction and bought it as a gift for her husband.

Over seventeen feet in length and weighing over two tons, the custom-made car used in the film was considered street legal and licensed to drive. According to *Hemmings Motor News*, it had a Ford V6 engine with automatic transmission. The wheels were molded in alloy to replicate the timber wheels of the period, and the boat deck was red-and-white cedar.

The license plate is GEN 11, signifying "genie," and, on a personal note, I own that same license plate, registered in Connecticut. Truly Scrumptious drives a yellow Humber 1909 with the license plate "CUB1," referring to producer Broccoli's nickname.

The Oscar-nominated musical score was written by Robert and Richard Sherman, who'd previously won for *Mary Poppins* —and the title song was used as a wake-up call for the Space Shuttle Discovery crew on November 7, 2007.

Other trivia: Lionel Jeffries, who plays the grandfather, was actually six months younger than Dick Van Dyke, whose character was named for Caractacus, the last independent ruler of England before the Roman Conquest. Baron Bomburst's castle is Neuschwanstein, built for Bavarian King Ludwig II between 1869 and 1886, and was the model for Disneyland's Sleeping Beauty's Castle.

On the Granger Movie Gauge of 1 to 10, *Chitty Chitty Bang Bang* is an engaging 8, a joyous romp for children of all ages.

Citizen Kane (RKO Radio Pictures) (1941)

If you poll movie critics and film historians, Orson Welles "Citizen Kane" not only comes out on the top of the list of influential American films but remains one of the most controversial, as it examines the life and legacy of megalomaniacal newspaper tycoon Charles Foster Kane (Welles), who lived as a recluse in Xanadu, his palatial estate in Florida.

Based on a script by Herman J. Mankiewicz, it was revised by Welles, who not only directed and starred but also had complete control of the final cut. Welles' techniques of dramatic structure, cinematography, special effects, makeup, sound and music were innovative, beginning with the non-linear story line which allowed him to reconstruct the character of Charles Foster Kane with fragments, like a metaphysical jigsaw puzzle, as seen through the eyes of the various people who had known him: his miserly childhood guardian (Georg Coulouris), best friend (Joseph Cotton), business manager (Everett Sloane), cynical butler (Paul Stewart), first wife (Ruth Warrick) and mistress/second wife (Dorothy Comingore). These flashbacks are revealed through the research of a journalist (William Alland) who is determined to solve the mystery of why Kane died holding a snow globe, uttering the word: "Rosebud."

In truth, Kane was based in part on Hearst but also on Chicago industrialist Samuel Insull, who married temperamental opera soprano Ganna Walska, and tycoon Harold Fowler McCormick, who built the Chicago Civic Opera House. And Welles often referred to the narrative search for the word's meaning as the "Rosebud" device, his own method of storytelling.

After seeing an advance preview, gossip columnist Louella Parsons deemed it "a repulsive biography" of her boss, William Randolph Hearst, who tried to bully RKO into shelving the project indefinitely and refused to acknowledge its release in his newspapers. When it opened in May, 1941, it was far from a hit, failing to recoup its cost at the box office. It wasn't until years later that its reputation was restored as European filmmakers like Federico Fellini, Max Ophuls, and Francois Truffaut acknowledged their debt to Welles' ingenuity.

Citizen Kane received nine Academy Award nominations but won only for Best Original Screenplay. Orson Welles was so unpopular in Hollywood that each time a *Citizen Kane* nominee's name was called out, the audience reportedly booed.

On the Granger Movie Gauge of 1 to 10, *Citizen Kane* is a superlative 10, a masterpiece.

City Lights (United Artists) (1931)

In 1931, after Hollywood became besotted with 'talkies' and no one else wanted to make silent films, Charlie Chaplin continued. He'd started work on "City Lights" in 1928 and, under pressure, composed a musical score and created several sound effects.

The story revolves around a Little Tramp (Chaplin) who falls in love with a blind flower girl (Virginia Cherrill). She mistakes him for a very wealthy man and, that night, he stops a drunken millionaire (Harry Myers) from drowning himself. Although he's rewarded, the eccentric millionaire only recognizes the Little Tramp as a friend when he's inebriated. While the Little Tramp works hard to raise the money needed for surgery in Vienna to restore the flower girl's sight, she still imagines that he's rich, so the dilemma becomes whether the girl will realize that her benevolent benefactor is the Little Tramp.

There are many stories about how Chaplin adopted the Little Tramp costume for which he became famous. In truth, it was derived from his studies of London street types: the moustache, immense trousers and huge shoes, worn on the wrong feet.

Contrasting the rich and poor, the theme is how that social status influences how you interpret what you see and hear. And the impact of Chaplin's pantomime on the development of comedy can hardly be exaggerated, as Charlie Chaplin imitators flourished, including young Bob Hope and Milton Berle.

A highlight which became one of Chaplin's most famous comic routines occurs when he's forced to get in the boxing ring with an opponent twice his size. And it's rumored that Chaplin re-shot the scene in which the Tramp buys a flower from the sightless girl 342 times, trying different ways to indicate that she thought he was affluent.

"More than machinery, we need humanity," Chaplin said. "More than cleverness, we need kindness and gentleness.... We want to live by each other's happiness, not by each other's misery. We don't want to hate and despise one another. In this world, there is room for everyone. And the good earth is rich and can provide for everyone."

Cover of the 1985 biography of Chaplin by David Robinson

On the Granger Movie Gauge of 1 to 10, *City Lights* is a poignantly touching 10, displaying Chaplin's genius for mixing comedy with pathos. No wonder that this was both Orson Welles' and Marlon Brando's favorite movie of all time.

Cocoon (20ᵗʰ Century-Fox) (1985)

Many explorers have searched for the fabled Fountain of Youth but who would have thought it was adjacent to a senior citizen home in St. Petersburg, Florida?

About 10,000 years ago, extraterrestrial explorers from the planet Antarea created an Earth outpost on the island of Atlantis. When Atlantis sank during an earthquake, 20 aliens remained behind, encased in silvery cocoons, to ensure that their brethren could return safely to their home planet. Now, four Antareans have returned to retrieve them from the bottom of the ocean.

Disguised as humans, they rent a boat from Jack Bonner (Steve Guttenberg) to retrieve the submerged cocoons which they deposit in a swimming pool that's been charged with Lifeforce to give their ancestors enough energy for the trip home. What the Antareans don't realize is that a group of elderly men has been routinely sneaking into that pool to swim – and they find the Lifeforce is miraculously revitalizing.

Arthur (Don Ameche), Ben (Wilfred Brimley) and Joe (Hume Cronyn) are the first to feel younger, stronger and happier, followed by Mary (Maureen Stapleton), Alma (Jessica Tandy) and Bess (Gwen Verdon). Only pessimistic Bernie (Jack Gilford) remains unconvinced. Eventually, the kindly alien leader (Brian Dennehy) offers these seniors a choice: stay on Earth, where they'll inevitably grow weaker and die, or travel with him to the distant planet of Antarea, where they'll remain rejuvenated – forever.

Loosely based on the novel by David Saperstein, Tom Benedeck's screenplay concentrates on the human drama, as directed by Ron Howard, who gave his wife, brother, mother and father small roles. He also cast Racquel Welch's daughter Tahnee and Tyrone Power's son, Tyrone Power Jr., since both bear strong resemblance to their famous parents.

Winning a Best Supporting Actor Oscar revived Don Ameche's career, and the cast returned for a sci-fi sequel *Cocoon: The Return* (1988). *Cocoon* also won a 1985 Oscar for Best Visual Effects. And if the music heard behind the Coast Guard's chase of Bonner's boat sounds familiar, it's the same composition that composer/conductor James Horner used in *Star Trek II: The Wrath of Khan* (1982), as Spock is trying to fix the warp drive.

> On the Granger Movie Gauge of 1 to 10, *Cocoon* is a poignant 10, resonating with tempting philosophical choices about immortality.

The Company Men (The Weinstein Company) (2010)

As relevant as today's headlines, this psychological drama is about several generations of executives pushed down the corporate ladder, forcing them to take jobs several rungs lower.

Beginning in the fall of 2008, thirtysomething sales exec Bobby Walker (Ben Affleck) discovers his future is going to be far more difficult than his past when he's 'downsized' out of Global Transportation Systems, a Boston-based ship-building firm. While he's still in denial, arrogantly driving his shiny Porsche and trying to sneak in a golf game at the country club, his savvy wife Maggie (Rosemary DeWitt) immediately begins reorganizing family expenditures, placing their heavily-mortgaged McMansion on the market, while his blue-collar brother-in-law Jack (Kevin Costner) urges him to consider joining his small company doing construction work.

Bobby's veteran co-worker Phil Woodward (Chris Cooper) sinks into deep despair when his pink slip comes, since he's considerably older and even more bewildered about the harsh realities of the bleak job market, particularly when his outplacement counselor glibly advises him to dye his gray hair, delete his Vietnam War service from his resume and not mention any jobs he's held before the 1990s.

Meanwhile, cantankerous Gene McClary (Tommy Lee Jones), the outspoken co-founder of the company, is ruthlessly dismissed by his best friend, cutthroat CEO James Salinger (Craig T. Nelson), who is only concerned about satisfying the shareholders. Ironically, while Gene's pretentious wife has been preoccupied with their palatial estate, corporate jet and luxurious holidays, he's been carrying on an affair with the glamorous GTS hatchet woman (Maria Bello).

First time feature-film writer/director John Wells (writer/producer of TV's *E.R.*) elicits intelligent, insightful performances from his acting ensemble which radiates fear, confusion, disbelief, disgust, anger and, finally, acceptance and, perhaps, hope. And cinematographer Roger Deakins visually captures the upper middle-class angst amidst the sleek offices and board rooms of the company's recently renovated headquarters.

On the Granger Movie Gauge of 1 to 10, *The Company Men* is a powerful, provocative, poignant 9, shrewdly reflecting the emotional savagery of the worldwide economic meltdown of the past three years.

The Curious Case of Benjamin Button (Paramount) (2008)

"I was born under unusual circumstances," explains Benjamin Button (Brad Pitt), who emerges from his dying mother's womb as a wrinkled old man. It's 1918, New Orleans, and his distraught father (Jason Flemyng) abandons the swaddled newborn on the doorstep of Nolan House, a retirement home, where he's taken in and lovingly raised by Queenie (Taraji P. Henson).

Despite his elderly infirmities, he's befriended by Daisy, a spirited young girl who often comes to visit her grandmother. While everyone else is growing older, Benjamin is gradually becoming younger. He goes to sea with rowdy tugboat Captain Mike (Jared Harris), who introduces him to worldly vices and pleasures. In the Russian port of Murmansk, Benjamin becomes infatuated with a sophisticated diplomat's wife, Elizabeth Abbot (Tilda Swinton), who dreams of swimming across the English Channel.

Meanwhile, Daisy (Cate Blanchett) has become a ballet dancer in New York. And when their lives once again intersect, they fall deeply in love, poignantly aware that their romantic relationship is doomed to be ephemeral, since Benjamin is living his life backwards. Inspired by F.Scott Fitzgerald's short story, screenwriter Eric Roth (*Forrest Gump*) cleverly frames Benjamin's epic fable into a gentle character-study, revolving around mortality, with haunting memories as related by elderly Daisy to her estranged daughter (Julia Ormond) in a New Orleans hospital during Hurricane Katrina.

Director David Fincher elicits subtly engaging performances, integrating Greg Cannom's miraculous make-up with Eric Barba's stunning visual effects and meticulous research by production designer Donald Graham Burt and costumer Jacqueline West.

At 167 minutes, it's too long, but on the Granger Movie Gauge of 1 to 10, *The Curious Case of Benjamin Button* is a tantalizing, touching, timeless 10. As Queenie says, "You never know what's coming for you."

The Dark Knight (Warner Bros.) (2008)

In the "Batman" movies, it's always the villains who steal the show—and Christopher Nolan's latest installment is no exception. Heath Ledger is dangerous and demented as the Joker, a cackling symbol of insane, unpredictable anarchy that's both timely and relevant in today's grim, chaotic world.

While billionaire Bruce Wayne/Batman (Christian Bale) has chased gangsters from Gotham City, the criminal community has rebelled, creating a far greater threat by turning to a villainous mastermind known as the Joker, whose cruel savagery is so unrelenting that he twists the souls of the Caped Crusader, District Attorney Harvey Dent (Aaron Eckhart) and Police Lieut. Jim Gordon (Gary Oldman).

"Criminals are complicated," observes Wayne's astute butler Alfred (Michael Caine). "Some men aren't looking for anything logical, like money. They can't be bought, bullied, reasoned or negotiated with. Some men just want to watch the world burn."

While it's macabre, even tragic, to watch Ledger (*Brokeback Mountain*) in his garish war paint, knowing that he died of a prescription drug overdose after filming ended, his malevolent performance has already generated talk of a posthumous Oscar, following in the footsteps of Peter Finch, who won in 1977 for *Network* two months after he died. And he's ably supported by brooding Bale, Caine, and Morgan Freeman, as Lucius Fox, who provides Wayne with high-tech gizmos and gadgets, like a Bat-suit and new two-wheeled Bat-Pod. Unfortunately, Maggie Gyllenhaal is given little to do but smile and shriek as Rachel Dawes.

Christopher Nolan (*Batman Returns, Memento*) —who wrote the script with his brother Jonathan—propels the action-filled crime drama at a brutal, frenetic, often confusing pace.

Yet on the Granger Movie Gauge of 1 to 10, The *Dark Knight* is a thrilling, terrifying 10. Once again, the Joker's wild!

The Dark Knight Rises (Warner Bros.) (2012)

Christopher Nolan saved the best for last, concluding the epic thrill-ogy that began with *Batman Begins* (2005) and continued with *The Dark Knight* (2008), re-imagining the iconic comic-book hero played by Christian Bale and making it relevant today.

Opening with a spectacular mid-flight sky-jacking of a CIA plane, the storyline picks up eight years after The Dark Knight was blamed for the death of popular District Attorney Harvey Dent and banished from Gotham City. Retreating in isolation to his mansion, Bruce Wayne has become a lonely recluse. "You're not living; you're just waiting," chides his faithful butler Alfred Pennyworth (Michael Caine).

But when he discovers an intrepid cat burglar, Selina Kyle (Anne Hathaway), rifling through his safe, Wayne's curiosity is piqued, particularly when she cautions, "There's a storm coming, Mr. Wayne." At the same time, a terrorist/thug named Bane (Tom Hardy) surfaces, wearing a mysterious, militaristic mask not to conceal his identity but to anesthetize himself against agonizing pain, resulting from injuries he suffered in prison. When compromised Commissioner Gordon (Gary Oldman) is hospitalized, he begs Batman to return, placing his trust in an idealistic, young protégé, Officer John Blake (Joseph Gordon-Levitt).

And wealthy philanthropist Miranda Tate (Marion Cotillard) becomes an influential ally when Wayne Enterprises, helmed by CEO/inventor Lucius Fox (Morgan Freeman), is the target of a hostile takeover. That's all you need to know—and all you should know—because, as the plot unravels, there are delicious surprises—spoilers—that no one should reveal.

Scripted by David S. Goyer, Jonathan Nolan and director Christopher Nolan, it's edge-of-the-seat exciting, ambiguously intriguing and emotionally involving – photographed by Wally Pfister and scored by Hans Zimmer.

Added to the Batcave arsenal, which includes the Batsuit, the Batmobile (a.k.a. The Tumbler) and the maneuverable, two-wheeled Bat-Pod, is a new airborne vehicle—part Apache attack helicopter/part Osprey prop jet/part Harrier jump jet—aptly named The Bat.

On the Granger Movie Gauge of 1 to1 0, *The Dark Knight Rises* is a triumphant 10. Tense and terrific—it's the best action-adventure of the summer!

The Day the Earth Stood Still (20th Century-Fox) (1951)

In the late 1970s when I taught screenwriting at the University of Bridgeport, most of my students were intoxicated by creating special effects. So I showed them this 1951 sci-fi classic to illustrate how—long before the digital age—skilled moviemakers created suspense, suspicion and fear. By today's standards, the special effects may be hokey but they're never cheesy.

Reflecting 1950s Cold War paranoia, a large, metallic spaceship lands on the Mall in Washington, D.C. Soldiers surround the craft as a helmeted humanoid figure emerges, announcing that he has come in peace, displaying a small object. When a nervous rifleman shoots him, his enormous robot guardian Gort appears, emitting a mysterious ray that melts the soldiers' weapons until the wounded alien orders him to desist.

Rushed to Walter Reed Hospital, Klaatu (Michael Rennie) tells presidential secretary Harley (Frank Conroy) that the object was a gift for the president and he's traveled over 250,000,000 miles to inform to Earth's leaders that the future of their planet is at stake. Sensing discord and fear, Klaatu escapes from the hospital and checks into a boarding house, where his encounters with various humans (Patricia Neal, Hugh Marlowe, Sam Jaffe, Billy Gray) teach him about our species.

Written by Edmund H. North, based on Harry Bates' short story "Farewell to the Master," directed with utmost realism by Robert Wise and punctuated by Bernard Herrmann's moody score, it contains several subtle, subliminal references to the Almighty Spirit, including having Klaatu assume the identity of a "Maj. Carpenter," rising from the dead and ascending into the sky. And the phrase "Klaatu barada nikto" has become part of popular culture.

Production designers Thomas Little and Claude Carpenter were inspired by architect Frank Lloyd Wright's Johnson Wax Headquarters, completed in 1936, for the alien craft and seven-foot-tall Lock Martin, an usher at Hollywood's Graumann's Chinese Theater, was outfitted in a metal suit to play Gort.

In 1985, President Ronald Reagan discussed uniting against an alien invasion when meeting Russia's President Mikhail Gorbachev; in 1987, Reagan told the United Nations: "I occasionally think how quickly our differences worldwide would vanish if we were facing an alien threat." As for the dreadful 2008 remake, starring Keanu Reeves, it is best ignored.

On the Granger Movie Gauge of 1 to 10, *The Day the Earth Stood Still* is a provocative 10. In 1995, it was selected for preservation in the United States National Film Registry.

The Departed (Warner Bros.) (2006)

Legendary director Martin Scorsese, a master of the gritty crime drama, has pulled out all the stops in this violent, blood-drenched tale of corruption. With its tangled web of intrigue and paranoia, it's reminiscent of *GoodFellas* and *Mean Streets*.

At the Massachusetts State Police Department, there are two young recruits, both with roots deep in the Irish-American community. Ambitious Colin Sullivan (Matt Damon) is chosen by the Elite Investigations Unit to help take down the local organized crime ring headed by powerful mob boss Frank Costello (Jack Nicholson).

But what the cops don't realize is that Sullivan's first loyalty, since childhood, has been to Costello. In contrast, there's hot-tempered, street-smart Billy Costigan (Leonardo DiCaprio), who ostensibly gets booted out of the police ranks but is, secretly, sent back onto the rough streets of South Boston to infiltrate Costello's inner-circle. Both are "moles" who, eventually, find out about one another – but not, ironically, through the risky relationship they share in common: a fondness for a particular police therapist (Vera Farmiga).

Sullivan and Costigan represent two sides of the same dented coin, each man choosing a different, but parallel path on a collision course littered with deception and betrayal.

Inspired by but not a remake of Hong Kong's *Infernal Affairs*, it's written with uncompromising film noir flair by William Monahan and wryly humorous input from Scorsese and Nicholson, who is astonishing and mesmerizing as the swaggering incarnation of evil. Nicholson dazzles! Leonardo DiCaprio captures the agony of Costigan's internal conflict, while Matt Damon gives Sullivan a tough core of intelligence.

On the Granger Movie Gauge of 1 to 10, *The Departed* is a tense, terrific 10. But there's a cautionary note in an unintended subliminal message: don't join the Massachusetts State Police Dept. if you hope to remain alive!

E.T.: The Extra-Terrestrial (Universal Studios) (1982)

Beginning with a poetically suspenseful introductory sequence, in which the tiny alien is accidentally abandoned in a California forest by a departing spaceship, this is the story of how a lonely, isolated young boy befriends the stranded extra-terrestrial, forming a mental, physical and emotional bond.

Written by Melissa Mathison from a child's perspective, the concept was based on an imaginary friend that director/producer Steven Spielberg created when his parents divorced in 1960. After hundreds of auditions, Spielberg chose ten-year-old Henry Thomas from San Antonio, Texas, to play Elliott and six-year-old Drew Barrymore, daughter of actors Ildiko Jade and John Drew Barrymore, as Elliott's mischievous little sister Gertie. In order to elicit convincing emotional performances from the youngsters, Spielberg filmed their scenes in roughly chronological order.

Originally, Elliott was to have lured E.T. into his suburban home with Milk Duds caramels, but M&Ms were substituted when Milk Duds' manufacturer balked; another switch was then made to Hershey's Reese's Pieces after M&M/Mars refused a massive pre-release sales drive. And it was Spielberg's colleague Robert Zemeckis who suggested having E.T. disguise himself as a stuffed animal in Elliott's closet.

Designed by Carlo Rambaldi, E.T.'s odd-looking face was inspired by the faces of Albert Einstein, Carl Sandberg and Ernest Hemingway. Two dwarves (Tamara De Treaux, Pat Bilon) and twelve-year-old Matthew De Meritt, who was born without legs, took turns wearing E.T.'s pint-sized costume, depending on which scene was being filmed, and professional mime Caprice Roth used prosthetics to play E.T.'s hands.

E.T. shares with many of Spielberg's films the theme of childhood, growing up and parental mortality. Refuting speculation that he'd intended it as a religious parable, Spielberg joked, "If I ever went to my (Jewish) mother and said, 'I've made this movie that's a Christian parable,' what do you think she'd say?' She has a kosher restaurant on Pico and Doheny in Los Angeles."

Nominated for nine Oscars in 1982, it was overwhelmed by the popularity of Richard Attenborough's biopic *Gandhi*, winning only four: Sound, Original Score, Visual Effects and Sound Effects Editing. And in Sweden, Finland and Norway, children under 12 were banned from seeing the film because of the "portrayal of adults as the enemies of children."

On the Granger Movie Gauge of 1 to 10, *E.T.: The Extra-Terrestrial* is a heart-warming 10, a lovable sci-fi masterpiece that's undoubtedly stood the test of time.

Ex-Machina (A24 Films) (2015)

Despite the hoopla over mega-franchise films, Alex Garland's sci-fi thriller is the most intriguing movie I've seen so far this year. As it begins, Caleb (Domhnall Gleeson), a geeky, twenty-four-year-old computer programmer, wins a company 'contest,' entitling him to spend a week at the remote Alaska estate belonging to his legendary boss, the brilliant-but-elusive billionaire Nathan Bateman (Oscar Isaac).

Arriving at the mountain retreat by helicopter, Caleb makes his way into Bateman's modernist, minimalist glass-and-steel compound; it's a high-tech research facility, much of which is subterranean.

An exercise/fitness fanatic, alcoholic Nathan tries to put him at ease, but Caleb is astounded by the Jackson Pollock paintings and other fine art, along with Kyoto (Sonoya Mizuno), a beautiful, silent servant.

Caleb's even more awestruck when he learns the purpose of his visit. He's to take part in the Turing Test, named for British artificial intelligence guru Alan Turing and referenced in *Blade Runner* —because Nathan has created what he believes is a sentient robot. Her name is Ava (Alicia Vikander).

Over the next few days, Caleb interacts with Ava, politely posing questions and evaluating her responses. As their sessions grow more and more ominous, the flirtatious, free-thinking android adapts to this stranger, slyly and seductively establishing the roots of a friendship and, perhaps, more.

That's all you need to know. Revealing more would ruin the surprises and dilute the suspense. Novelist-turned-screenwriter Alex Garland (*28 Days Later*, *Sunshine*) makes an auspicious directing debut in this chilling exploration of the human psyche – in a style eerily reminiscent of Stanley Kubrick.

Working on a $13 million budget, kudos to production designer Mark Digby, costumer Sammy Sheldon Differ and cinematographer Rob Hardy. A fun fact about Domhnall Gleeson, also seen in *Harry Potter and the Deathly Hallows*, is that he is the son of Irish actor Brendan Gleeson; he's starring in George Lucas' upcoming *Star Wars*. Oscar Isaac is best known for *Inside Llewyn Davis* and *A Most Violent Year*, while Swedish actress Alicia Vikander is an ex-ballerina, last seen in *Anna Karenina*, and *A Royal Affair*.

On the Granger Movie Gauge of 1 to 10, *Ex-Machina* is an intense, mind-melding 9, derived from the Greek phrase "Deus ex machina," or "god from the machine," referring to a dramatic, problem-solving plot device.

Finding Nemo (Disney) (2003)

There should be nothing fishy about the success of this underwater adventure. It's got everything going for it: intriguing anthropomorphic characters, a compelling story and fanciful computer-generated animation. Set in and around Australia's Great Barrier Reef, it's the tale of Marlin (voiced by an anxious Albert Brooks), a neurotic, overprotective father clownfish, who is searching for Nemo (Alexander Gould), his son who was 'taken' by a deep-sea diving dentist.

Marlin and his friendly-but-forgetful regal blue tang fish companion Dory (Ellen DeGeneres) must confront perils ranging from scary whales, pink jellyfish, predatory sharks and surfer-dude turtles to sunken ships, deadly mines and dangerous ocean currents ("the swirling vortex of terror"). Honest, heartfelt emotion ebbs and flows along with humor—both low (the inevitable burp/fart jokes) and high (allusions to Alcoholics Anonymous, Alfred Hitchcock, etc.) —plus fluid vocal contributions from Willem Dafoe, Geoffrey Rush, Allison Janney, Brad Garrett, Barry Humphries, Austin Pendleton and Andrew Stanton (the film's director).

The theme is to trust your child enough to let go and to allow him make his own mistakes—with a subplot involving overcoming physical challenges, since little Nemo has a tiny, underdeveloped fin. With its four features— *Toy Story*, *A Bug's Life*, *Toy Story 2*, *Monsters, Inc.*, now this—Pixar Animation sets a digital high water mark for eye-candy and is, quite simply, the best in the business today. Thomas Newman's music and Gary Rydstrom's sound effects are superb, and there's no more fitting final credit song than "Beyond the Sea," sung by Robbie Williams.

On the Granger Movie Gauge of 1 to 10, *Finding Nemo* is a fun, bubbly, fantastic 10. Sea it!

Flags of Our Fathers
(Paramount Pictures) (2006)

Two-time Oscar-winning director Clint Eastwood explores the story behind the most memorable photograph of World War II—and not since *Saving Private Ryan* has a historical wartime epic packed this kind of powerful emotional wallop.

On February 23, 1945, Associated Press photographer Joe Rosenthal snapped a picture of five Marines and one Navy Corpsman raising the U.S. flag on Mount Suribachi after a bloody, horrific 35-day battle in which 6,821 American soldiers were killed and 20,000 more were wounded. "Raising the Flag on Iwo Jima" made instant heroes of the random men in the picture. So, manipulated by the military, the three surviving flag-raisers (Ryan Phillippe, Jesse Bradford, Adam Beach) became an integral part of the government's War Bond Tour. Trapped in the exploitive spotlight of symbolic adulation, they soon realized that the glory of celebrity fades fast, followed by disappointment and disillusionment.

Based on the best-seller by James Bradley with Ron Powers, the screenplay by William Broyles Jr. (*Apollo 13*) and Paul Haggis (*Crash*) reveals the fighting that led up to the photograph and what happened to the men after they returned home. Within their psychological conflict is justifiable skepticism of the mythology of hero-worship.

Produced by Steven Spielberg and directed by Clint Eastwood (who also composed the musical score), there's a spectacular visual scope although the complex, non-linear structure presents a challenge for the audience. Cinematographer Tom Stern fades out colors, often moving monochromatically between chaos and coherence—and the actors, particularly Adam Beach (*Windtalkers*), acquit themselves admirably.

On the Granger Movie Gauge of 1 to 10, *Flags of Our Fathers* is a compelling 10—to be followed, by Eastwood's *Letters from Iwo Jima*, delving into the battle from the Japanese perspective.

Frequency (New Line Cinema) (2000)

O nce you see this movie, you can't stop thinking about it. *Frequency* poses the question: What if you could travel back in time and change your past? That's the dilemma that faces NYPD Detective John Sullivan (John Caviezel) who discovers that, while using an old ham radio just when a natural phenomenon, an aurora borealis, is lighting up the night sky, he is actually talking with a man who died 30 years earlier – his own father. Back in 1969, his dad, Frank Sullivan (Dennis Quaid), was killed fighting a warehouse fire. But what if John could warn his father and, thereby, save his life? It's worth a try, isn't it? But, then, if it works, the past is inexorably changed, so what happens to the present? That's all I'm going to tell you about the plot.

Like *The Sixth Sense*, this is not a movie you want to know too much about. Toby Emmerich has written a stunning, multi-layered thriller that's part murder mystery, involving a serial killer, part family drama, revolving around the loving relationship of father and son. Science-fiction time-travel fantasy goes back to Jules Verne and H.G. Wells, and Emmerich's imaginative contribution is cutting-edge.

Credibility is maintained and continuity matches, despite the complicated plot twists and mind-bending paradoxes involving temporal intersections with parallel universes. Director Gregory Hoblit (*Primal Fear*) keeps the action fast-paced and the tension taut, shooting the ham radio scenes like a live, multi-camera TV show. What's on the screen is totally entertaining, emotionally gripping, and so thought-provoking that you may want to see it twice.

On the Granger Movie Gauge of 1 to 10, *Frequency* is an exciting, surprising 10. If you're into edge-of-the-seat suspense pulling the cosmic strings of time travel, *Frequency* will light your fuse.

From Here to Eternity
(Columbia Pictures) (1953)

Based on James Jones' best-seller, the story is set at Honolulu's Schofield Army Barracks in the summer of 1941, prior to the surprise Japanese attack on Pearl Harbor.

When Private Robert E. Lee Prewitt (Montgomery Clift) is transferred from the Bugle Corps at Fort Shafter to Rifle Company G, he's recruited for the regimental boxing club by Captain Dana "Dynamite" Holmes (Philip Ober), who promises that he will be promoted to corporal, even sergeant if he helps win the boxing trophy on December 15. But Prewitt refuses. Holmes retaliates by making Prewitt's life miserable, hoping to break his resolve. When that fails, he orders First Sergeant Milton Warden (Burt Lancaster) to prepare court martial papers.

Other non-commissioned officers assist in the vicious cruelty against Prewitt, whose only friend is Private Angelo Maggio (Frank Sinatra). Meanwhile, Warden ignites an affair with Holmes' wife Karen (Deborah Kerr), as Prewitt falls in love with bar hostess Alma "Lorene" Burke (Donna Reed) to whom he confides that the reason he refuses to box is because he accidentally blinded a close friend while sparring. And ill-fated Maggio makes an enemy of Staff Sergeant "Fatso" Judson (Ernest Borgnine) who brutally abuses him in the stockade.

Screenwriter Daniel Taradash toned down the book's explicit sex, bawdy language and sadism, while developing the dramatic character study which concludes on the fateful morning of December 7th. As vice-president in charge of production, my father, S. Sylvan Simon, worked with director Fred Zinnemann, convincing studio executive Harry Cohn to cast Frank Sinatra, Deborah Kerr and Donna Reed in roles that changed their careers. After my father's sudden death, Buddy Adler took over as producer.

Stories that Frank Sinatra got the part because of alleged mob connections are untrue but his cause certainly benefitted from Eli Wallach's turning it down to appear in *Camino Real* on Broadway instead. The scene in which Prew meets Maggio and Lorene in the bar after he walks off guard duty was actually Sinatra's screen test - and he improvised, using olives as dice, pretending to shoot craps. Opening to rave reviews, *From Here to Eternity* was not only one of 1953's top money-makers but one of the 10 highest-grossing films of the decade. Nominated for 13 Academy Awards, it won eight, including Picture, Director, Screenplay, Supporting Actor (Sinatra), Supporting Actress (Reed), Cinematography, Editing and Sound. And the erotically-charged beach scene was audacious and innovative at the time.

On the Granger Movie Gauge of 1 to 10, *From Here to Eternity* is a tough, starkly realistic 10 - considered by many to be a much better motion picture than the novel was as a book.

Galaxy Quest (DreamWorks) (1999)

Glory, Hallelujah—this is the Christmas action comedy you've been waiting for! Tim Allen, Sigourney Weaver, Alan Rickman, Tony Shalhoub, and Daryl Mitchell play five actors who—20 years ago—starred on a popular television series that was canceled. For four seasons, from 1979 to 1982, they played the crew of the NSEA Protector—now they earn their living appearing in costume at sci-fi conventions and chain-store openings.

However, far in deep, outer space, the Thermians, a race of aliens from the Klatu Nebula, have intercepted Earth's TV transmissions and, having no knowledge of fiction or drama, they have mistaken the sci-fi shows for valid historical documents. So when they're faced with a deadly adversary, the ruthless Roth'h'ar Sarris of Fatu-Krey (Robin Sachs), the Thermians abduct the characters – Comdr. Peter Quincy Taggert, Lt. Tawny Madison, Dr. Lazarus, et. al. —not realizing they're really out-of-work actors. With no script, no director, and no clue about real space travel, the actors must turn in the performances of their lives to become the intergalactic heroes they've convinced everyone they are, as they encounter cannibalistic Blue Demon children, a giant Rock Monster, and a Pig Lizard.

As the vain, self-serving commander, Tim Allen has never been better. Sigourney Weaver is a sexy, shameless babe, and Alan Rickman is outrageous as a Shakespearean-trained Brit who has been reduced to playing a half-human/half reptile.

On the Granger Movie Gauge of 1 to 10, *Galaxy Quest* is an exuberant, enormously funny 8. Aptly directed by Dean Parisot from a cleverly ironic screenplay by David Howard and Robert Gordon, it's a bright, shiny holiday package of pure enjoyment, destined to blast into one of the big hits of the season.

God Grew Tired of Us (Newmarket/ National Geographic Films) (2006)

Perhaps you've heard about the 27,000 boys, some as young as five, who fled Sudan when the Arab-Muslim north attacked the Christian, or animistic, south in 1983. In 1987, the Islamic fundamentalist government decreed it would kill all male children in the south. Many were burned in their homes. In terror, these boys, mostly from the Dinka tribe, fled on foot through more than 1,000 miles of sub-Saharan wilderness.

About 12,000 made it to the Kokuma Refugee Camp in Kenya, where they've lived for more than 15 years, away from their families, forming their own fraternal bonds. This documentary focuses on three of these "lost boys" —John Bul Dau, Panther Bior and Daniel Abol Pach—now young men, who were allowed to immigrate to the United States.

While they're often awed by the marvels of electricity, toilets, apartments and supermarkets and always grateful, they're also saddened by the lonely, alienated American lifestyle. Astonishingly eloquent, they articulate how they miss the close-knit group support as they adjust to this new, highly individualistic culture. In their spiritual values, kindness and consideration are of utmost importance, even with strangers.

One of their friends, we're told, becomes mentally ill and must be institutionalized. But these three survive their relocation, struggle to get an education, and consistently send money back to friends and family in Africa, determined to help others from their homeland attain a better life.

Filmmaker Christopher Quinn utilizes archival footage to set the tone, as narrator Nicole Kidman provides connective continuity.

On the Granger Movie Gauge of 1 to 10, *God Grew Tired of Us* is an inspiring 10, proving that the American Dream is still alive and that the human spirit is, indeed, indomitable.

The Godfather (Paramount Pictures) (1972)

As the first blockbuster of the 1970s, this gangster picture became the biggest-grossing film at that time, winning acclaim throughout the world. With a budget of $6 million and a then-unknown director, it was a gamble—one that richly paid off.

In the life of Don Corleone (Marlon Brando), his Sicilian/New York family comes first. Ruthless when he's not respected, the patriarch does not condone drugs, so when a drug dealer, Virgil Sollozzo (Al Lettieri), approaches him for protection, offering a percentage of the profits, the Don turns him down. Infuriated, Sollozzo has him shot. At that point, despite his initial reluctance, the Don's beloved youngest son Michael (Al Pacino) begins a violent mob war involving organized crime's Five Families—The Tattaglias, The Barzinis, The Cuneos and The Straccis - which tears the Corleone family apart.

Based on a pulpy screenplay by Mario Puzo, it's directed by Francis Ford Coppola, who explored the dramatically rich subtext when he was scouting locations in Italy with cinematographer Gordon Willis. As an ensemble piece, the part of Michael is pivotal. Although Coppola wanted Al Pacino, who looked Italian-American, Paramount executive Robert Evans didn't think he looked like a movie star and kept referring to him as "that little dwarf," so Warren Beatty, Robert De Niro, Jack Nicholson, Ryan O'Neal, Robert Redford, Martin Sheen, Dustin Hoffman, even Alain Delon were considered.

Eventually, a huge cast was chosen, including James Caan, John Cazale, Robert Duvall, Talia Shire, Diane Keaton, Al Martino and Richard Conte (whom Martin Scorsese's Sicilian mother asked Coppola to use). The lead actors were paid only $35,000 each, with Brando receiving $50,000, with some net points. Coppola received $110,000 and six points (6% of the net).

Coppola recalled: "*The Godfather* was a very unappreciated movie when we were making it...I was always on the verge of getting fired. So it was an extremely nightmarish experience...I wasn't at all confident that it was going to be successful and that I'd ever get another job." One of the most memorable moments involves the real severed head of a horse, and when animal rights groups protested, Coppola swore the head was delivered from a dog food company and that the animal had not been killed specifically for the movie. In 1972, *The Godfather* was Oscar-nominated in seven categories and won three Academy Awards: Best Picture, Actor (Brando) and Adapted Screenplay. It then spawned two sequels.

On the Granger Movie Gauge of 1 to10, *The Godfather* is an almost mythological 10, touching on universal themes of power, money, loyalty and violence.

Gone With the Wind (Selznick International/M.G.M.) (1939)

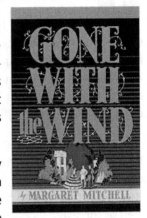

Adapted from Margaret Mitchell's novel of the Old South, this lavish Technicolor epic is one of the most popular and profitable pictures of all time. Vivien Leigh embodies the high-spirited, indomitable heroine, Scarlett O'Hara, adoring gentlemanly Ashley Wilkes (Leslie Howard) and crushed when he chooses to marry altruistic Melanie (Olivia de Havilland). Spurned, Scarlett weds two other men who die during the Civil War before she meets her match in strong, shrewd Rhett Butler (Clark Gable).

Meticulously produced by David O. Selznick, scripted by Sidney Howard (with assistance from Jo Swerling, Ben Hecht and John Van Druten) and directed by Victor Fleming (plus un-credited George Cukor and Sam Wood), it premiered on December 15, 1939, at the racially segregated Fox Theater in Atlanta, Georgia, where supporting actress Hattie McDaniel was pointedly excluded. Later, McDaniel became not only the first black performer to win an Academy Award but also the first to attend the celebratory Oscar banquet as a guest rather than a waitress.

Garnering a total of 10 Oscars, including a Special Award for "mood enhancement" to production designer William Cameron Menzies and the Irving Thalberg Award to Selznick – "GWTW" set an Oscar-winning record that lasted 20 years.

It's Hollywood mythology that Clark Gable's celebrated closing line—"Frankly, my dear, I don't give a damn"—was the first occasion on which the word 'damn' was used on the screen; it had been used several times before. But this film did set a record for the most extensive screen tests for the part of Scarlett with Jean Arthur, Joan Bennett, Paulette Goddard as final contenders. Indeed, the movie went into production before green-eyed, British actress Vivien Leigh copped the coveted role after visiting the 'burning of Atlanta' set with David's brother, Myron Selznick. And it's true that Clark Gable refused to shed tears on-screen, citing weeping as both 'unmanly' and unseemly for the star known as Tinsel Town's 'King.'

On the Granger Movie Gauge of 1 to 10, *Gone With the Wind* is a triumphant 10. Taking inflation into account, it remains the biggest moneymaker in the history of American cinema.

The Green Mile (Warner Bros.) (1999)

Based on Stephen King's best-seller, it's set on Death Row in a Southern prison in 1935 - and was nominated for four Academy Awards.

The title refers to the stretch of lime-colored linoleum from the cell block to the electric chair. Tom Hanks plays the head guard who recalls, in flashback, his poignant, mystical friendship with an unusual prisoner, a black man with a mysterious, supernatural gift. This massive, seven-foot tall inmate, played by Michael Clarke Duncan, was convicted of the rape and murder of two little girls, yet his naive nature and gentle demeanor not only raise questions about his guilt but also about the inexplicable nature of miracles.

As in every fable, there has to be a villain. In this case, there are two: Doug Hutchison, as Hanks' sadistic subordinate, and Sam Rockwell, as a vicious serial killer. And there are three executions. The second is so boldly horrifying that the words like gruesome and gory seem trivial. But there's also humor and, in a very visceral sense, the audience participates every step of the way.

Writer-director Frank Darabont's casting is meticulous. Hanks and Duncan, in particular, deliver extraordinary performances, along with James Cromwell, Michael Jeter, and Patricia Clarkson. Nothing is perfect—the bookending device used at the beginning and end is weak – but who cares? Perhaps the biggest advantage of making a great film like this is knowing what not to worry about.

On the Granger Movie Gauge of 1 to 10, *The Green Mile* is a compelling, powerful 10. Nothing can prepare you for the suspenseful grip this haunting story holds—and the chilling gamble that must be taken. An absolute masterpiece, it's one of the best movies of the year.

The Harry Potter Movies (Warner Bros.) (2001-2011)

The eight screen adaptations of J.J. Rowling's fun-filled *Harry Potter* best-selling novels form the most successful franchise in cinema history.

Harry Potter and the Sorcerer's Stone introduces impish, bespectacled eleven-year-old Harry Potter (Daniel Radcliffe) who – on his 11th—birthday learns that he's a wizard. Years ago, as an infant with a scar on his forehead, he was deposited in Surrey on the doorstep of his aunt and uncle, the Dursleys (Richard Griffiths, Fiona Shaw); these distrustful "muggles" (mere mortals) forced him to sleep in a cupboard below the stairs. So when Harry is whisked off to Hogwarts School of Witchcraft and Wizardry, his entire life changes. He befriends brilliant if bossy Hermione Granger (Emma Watson) and wry, irreverent Ron Weasley (Rupert Grint), as the three embark on incredible adventures to thwart the evil intentions of the Lord Voldemort (Ralph Fiennes).

This character-driven fantasy continues through *Harry Potter and the Chamber of Secrets, Harry Potter and the Prisoner of Azkaban, Harry Potter and the Goblet of Fire, Harry Potter and the Order of the Phoenix, Harry Potter and the Half-Blood Prince* and *Harry Potter and the Deathly Hallows, Parts 1 & 2.*

What's extraordinary is how producer David Heyman, screenwriter Steve Kloves, production designer Stuart Craig and various directors have not only explored the classic good vs. evil themes of loyalty and love, friendship and understanding, but also cinematically chronicled how these innocent, often bewildered youngsters have evolved into bright, brave, resourceful, albeit flawed, young adults. As the children grew up, so has the audience.

The predominantly British cast includes Jim Broadbent, Helena Bonham Carter, John Cleese, Robbie Coltrane, Warwick Davis, Michael Gambon, Brendan Gleeson, Richard Harris, John Hurt, Jason Isaacs, Bill Nighy, Gary Oldman, Alan Rickman, Maggie Smith, Timothy Spall, Imelda Staunton, David Thewlis, Emma Thompson and Julie Walters, among others; a record 13 actors have appeared as the same character in all eight films.

Except for Chris Columbus, each director did a cameo. Alfonzo Cuaron is a wizard holding a candle in *Prisoner of Azkaban*, in which producer David Heyman can be glimpsed within a moving portrait. Mike Newell is heard as a radio presenter in *Goblet of Fire*. And David Yates is a wizard within a moving portrait in *Order of the Phoenix*.

On the Granger Movie Gauge of 1 to 10, *The Harry Potter* movies are a triumphant 10— with an epilogue tying the final knot in the narrative thread of this spellbinding series.

The Help (DreamWorks/Disney) (2011)

Adroitly adapted from Kathryn Stockett's controversial 2009 novel, it's the very personal story of three women in Jackson, Mississippi, in the early 1960s. Ambitious Eugenia 'Skeeter' Phelan (Emma Stone), an Ole Miss grad, wants to be an author and, while she lands a job ghostwriting a 'cleaning advice' column for the local newspaper, a New York book editor (Mary Steenburgen) says she can only succeed if she writes something personal – and timely.

Knowing little about cleaning, Skeeter seeks advice from her friend's maid Aibileen (Viola Davis), but chatting with hired help doesn't sit well with the brittle belles of the segregationist bridge club. So inquisitive Skeeter goes out, secretly, at night, to Aibileen's house and begins to question what it feels like to be a black servant, taking care of white people's babies. After all, Aibileen's raised 17 white children, often becoming their surrogate mother. Aibileen's understandably reluctant at first but soon she's sharing her suffering, including how her only son was killed by racist negligence after a mill accident.

This kind of fraternization not only breaks Southern societal rules but also puts them at risk of the law. But soon Aibileen's saucy, outspoken friend Minny (Octavia Spencer) decides to confide in open-minded Skeeter, as do a dozen other maids, telling their poignant tales of domestic life, particularly mistreatment by perky Southern replicas of Betty Draper in TV's "Mad Men."

Like Hilly (Bryce Dallas Howard), a malicious racist whose spitefulness offends everyone, including her mother (Sissy Spacek); Elizabeth (Ahna O'Reilly), who deliberately neglects her plump, toddler daughter; Skeeter's own ailing mother (Allison Janney) who inexplicably fired their beloved, longtime maid Constantine (Cicily Tyson); and hapless Celia (Jessica Chastain), a shunned newcomer who's considered "white trash."

Adapted and directed by Kathryn Stockett's observant childhood friend Tate Taylor, it resounds with sensitive emotional truth, even if it's episodic and uneven, lacking subtlety. The acting ensemble is superb, particularly Viola Davis and scene-stealing Octavia Spencer.

On the Granger Movie Gauge of 1 to 10, *The Help* is a provocative, powerful 9, a multi-racial, multi-generational 'must see.'

High Noon (Columbia Pictures) (1952)

While Gary Cooper's stardom was indelibly associated with Westerns, none of his portrayals was more memorable than that of Will Kane, the longtime marshal of Hadleyville in the New Mexico Territory. Having just married Amy (Grace Kelly), a pacifist Quaker, Kane turns in his badge, intending to move away and become a store-keeper. But before he can leave, he learns that Frank Miller (Ian MacDonald), a criminal he'd brought to justice, is due to arrive on the noon train – and wreak revenge. Unsuccessful in eliciting help from the terrorized townsfolk, Kane is trapped in moral and emotional turmoil, particularly when Amy issues an ultimatum: she's leaving on the noon train – with or without him.

Based on John W. Cunningham's story *The Tin Star*, the screenplay was written by Carl Foreman and directed by Fred Zinneman to take place in the exact screening time of the film – less than 90 minutes.

Gary Cooper's daughter Maria, with whom I grew up, recalls how this film evoked memories of his own father. She quotes Cooper as saying, "When Stanley Kramer sent me the script, I saw in it the graphic presentation of everything I'd learned at home. As a trial lawyer and later a judge in the Montana Supreme Court, my father knew sheriffs all over the West, and he knew what they were up against. Law enforcement, as he taught me, was everybody's job. The sheriff was not a lone figure, but the representative of the people's desires for law and order, and unless he had the people behind him, he was in poor shape. Such a man was the sheriff I was asked to portray."

High Noon garnered seven 1952 Oscar nominations, including Best Picture, but was defeated by Cecil B. DeMille's circus-themed *The Greatest Show on Earth* for what many cite as political reasons, since writer/producer Carl Foreman was declared "an uncooperative witness' by Sen. Joe McCarthy's House Un-American Activities Committee (HUAC) and subsequently black-listed.

Since Cooper was scheduled to be in Europe during the ceremonies, John Wayne accepted his Academy Award as Best Actor. Sung by Tex Ritter (father of actor John Ritter), Dimitri Tiomkin's theme song— "Do Not Forsake Me, Oh, My Darlin'" —became a huge hit.

On the Granger Movie Gauge of 1 to 10, *High Noon* is a time-ticking 10, and it's been cited as the favorite film of U.S. Presidents Dwight D. Eisenhower and Bill Clinton.

Hope Springs (Columbia Pictures/Sony) (2012)

Omaha suburbanites Kay (Meryl Streep) and Arnold (Tommy Lee Jones) have been married for 31 years, and their comfortable Nebraska nest is empty—in more ways than one. Although she timidly ventures from her bedroom to his in an enticing negligee, he's too engrossed in GOLF magazines to notice; that's the way it's been for the past five years. While she yearns for connection, he's completely closed off.

Working part-time at Coldwater Creek, Kay hears about a week-long couple's counseling retreat in Great Hope Springs, Maine, that's hosted by a celebrated pop-psychology therapist. Desperate in her loneliness, she spends $4,000 from her savings to sign them up. Although Arnold, who's a cheapskate accountant, initially balks, he reluctantly joins her—in body, if not in spirit. So it's up to Dr. Bernie Feld (Steve Carell) to gently coax them into communicating with each other and re-establishing sexual intimacy.

After honing her expertise on HBO's sexy couples-therapy drama *Tell Me You Love Me*, Vanessa Taylor's script is loaded with heart, soul and laughs which director David Frankel handles with the same kind of candid, realistic honesty and intelligence that made his previous collaboration with Streep on *The Devil Wears Prada* so hilarious.

Both Streep and Jones are flat-out fabulous. She imbues Kay with warm determination and aching vulnerability, while Jones's Arnold is a stubborn, cantankerous curmudgeon who has been stifling his emotions for years and is averse to letting his guard down. (Reportedly, Jeff Bridges originally turned down the part which is how it – luckily - landed in Jones' lap.)

To his credit, Carell (*The 40-Year-Old Virgin*) plays it not only straight but his calm, compassionate empathy with their nervousness and fear is quite convincing. Elisabeth Shue, Jean Smart and Mimi Rogers also contribute memorable turns.

For locals who may recognize the scenery, Norwalk, Guilford and Stonington, Connecticut, stood in for coastal Maine.

On the Granger Movie Gauge of 1 to 10, *Hope Springs* is a heart-warming, irreverent, uplifting 8, a downright funny, feel-good, romantic comedy/drama for adults.

House of Flying Daggers (Sony Pictures Classics) (2004)

If you've never seen a martial arts extravaganza like *Crouching Tiger, Hidden Dragon*, then Zhang Yimou's newest epic adventure will thrill you. But, frankly, I preferred his previous film, the visually dazzling "Hero," which was finally released late this summer after a long delay.

Set in China in the ninth century, amid the corruption of the Tang Dynasty, this story centers on an underground political rebellion run by a secret society of Robin Hood-esque assassins known as the House of Flying Daggers.

The complicated, convoluted plot involves three characters: two police captains (Japanese-Taiwanese actor Takeshi Kaneshiro and Hong Kong's Andy Lau) and a graceful yet formidable blind dancer (China's superstar Zhang Ziyi), a courtesan at a house of pleasure called the Peony Pavilion—although no one is what he/she seems to be. Writer/director Zhang Yimou (*Raise the Red Lantern, Ju Dou*) discards his charming, lyrical mysticism in favor of a straightforward narrative and cleverly choreographed "wuxia" (chivalry and swordplay).

There's also an innovative, intriguing interlude, called The Echo Game, that involves agile dancing and intricate drumming. While Zhao Xiaoding's lush rural landscape cinematography is impeccable, particularly when it captures autumn's change into winter, the duplicitous love triangle never develops any emotional depth. And enough with the conventional flying/fighting in the bamboo forest!

What was astounding at first has now become a stylized cliché– and the crescent-shaped, gravity-defying flying daggers are all-too-obviously CGI.

Nevertheless, on the Granger Movie Gauge of 1 to 10, *House of Flying Daggers* is an awesome 8, culminating with operatic soprano Kathleen Battle singing the theme song, "Lovers."

How Green Was My Valley (20th Century-Fox) (1941)

Based on Richard Llewellyn's 1939 childhood memoir about life in the coal-mining valleys of Wales, this is one of the most warmly sympathetic depictions of the social themes of the Depression: "Strange that the mind will forget so much of what only this moment has passed, and yet hold clear and bright the memory of what happened years ago, of men and women long since dead," says the narrator.

Huw (Roddy McDowall) is the youngest child of Gwilym (Donald Crisp) and Beth (Sara Allgood) Morgan. While his older brothers work deep in the mines with their father, his sister Angharad (Maureen O'Hara) helps keep house. Although Angharad loves the preacher, Mr. Gruffydd (Walter Pidgeon), he can't bear to subject her to an impoverished churchman's life, so she marries the mine owner's son and moves away. Eventually, socio-economics changes everything in the Rhondda Valley.

Defiantly produced by Darryl F. Zanuck on a budget of only $1 million, it's the gripping tale of a family beset by poverty and its heroic efforts to survive. The original director, William Wyler, chose young Roddy McDowall for the lead but Wyler was eventually replaced by director John Ford (*The Grapes of Wrath*, *Tobacco Road*, *Drums Along the Mohawk*) who had hoped to film in Wales. But W.W. II made that impossible, so craftsmen built an exact replica of the mining town at the Fox Ranch in Malibu Canyon.

What's fascinating is how Philip Dunne's screen adaptation adroitly managed to evade the book's most controversial element: the labor vs. management battle in connection with the miners' strike. Instead, Huw simply says: "Everything I ever learnt as a small boy came from my father...The simple lessons he taught me are sharp and clear in my mind as if I had heard them only yesterday... Men like my father cannot die. They are with me still, real in memory as they were in flesh, loving and beloved forever. How green was my valley then."

On the Granger Movie Gauge of 1 to 10, *How Green Was My Valley* is a melancholy 9. It was so popular that it won Best Picture at the Academy Awards, defeating major contenders like Orson Welles' *Citizen Kane*, Howard Hawks's *Sergeant York* and William Wyler's *The Little Foxes*. It also won Oscars for Directing, Screenwriting, Cinematography, Editing, Music, Set Design, Sound, Best Supporting Actor (Donald Crisp) and Best Supporting Actress (Sara Allgood).

Hugo (Paramount Pictures) (2011)

Martin Scorsese brings Brian Selznick's beloved children's book, *The Invention of Huge Cabret*, to life in this magical adventure, gloriously filmed in 3-D and set in a busy Parisian train station in the 1930s.

Living with his dissolute uncle (Ray Winstone) in a tiny apartment secreted in the walls in the station's rafters, Hugo Cabret (Asa Butterfield) is an intrepid twelve-year-old orphan who oils and maintains the station's clocks. His prize possession is a broken-down automaton and a notebook, left by his father (Jude Law), containing complicated instructions about how to repair the intricate, wind-up robotic figure.

Cleverly eluding the watchful Inspector (Sasha Baron Cohen) and his Doberman, Hugo stealthily steals the tiny parts he needs from cranky toy-store proprietor Georges Melies (Ben Kingsley), who eventually catches him.

Because he fears that his precious notebook will be burned, Hugo dares to leave the station and follow Melies home, where he befriends his goddaughter Isabelle (Chloe Grace Moretz) and discovers that embittered Melies is a magician-turned- pioneer filmmaker who once worked in an awesome glass studio, creating 500 incredible sci-fi fantasies, the most famous of which was *A Trip to the Moon* (1902). Indeed, visionary Georges Melies (1861-1938) was the first filmmaker to recognize the connection between the cinema and dreams.

Director Martin Scorsese, cinematographer Robert Richardson and set designer Dante Ferretti have integrated not only fanciful impressions of French visual culture, including Dadaism and the short films of Man Ray, Leger, Rene Clair, and the Lumiere brothers, but also richly detailed remnants of the Mechanical Age, including the clocks and the trains, particularly the locomotives.

Deserving recognition are Sandy Powell's costumes, Rob Legato's visual effects, John Logan's adaptation, Thelma Schoonmaker's editing and Howard Shore's musical score—along with the superb acting ensemble, including Helen McCrory, Emily Mortimer and Christopher Lee. Artfully integrated into the concept is Scorsese's passionate plea for the preservation of film, the most innovative art form of the 20th century.

On the Granger Movie Gauge of 1 to 10, *Hugo* is an opulent, dazzling, enchanting 10. It's family-friendly fun.

The Hunger Games (Lionsgate) (2012)

How well does this movie accomplish what it sets out to do? That's the primary question that propels my writing each review. In cinematically adapting the first of Suzanne Collins's young adult novels, the answer is superbly.

In a dystopian future, a post-apocalyptic country called Panem, which was once North America, is divided into 12 districts. As annual penance for an anti-government uprising 74 years earlier, each district holds a 'reaping' in which a teenage girl and boy are selected to participate as Tributes in a televised, high-tech sacrificial slaughter known as the Hunger Games, during which only one competitor survives.

When her terrified younger sister is chosen, sixteen-year-old Katniss Everdeen (Jennifer Lawrence) impulsively volunteers to take her place, representing impoverished, coal-mining District 12, presumably Appalachia, along with the baker's son, Peeta Mellark (Josh Hutcherson). En route to the garish, candy-colored Capitol, they meet their mentor, drunken, dissolute Haymitch Abernathy (Woody Harrelson), a former victor. After a brief indoctrination, grueling evaluation and sycophantic beauty pageant-like interviews, the pubescent gladiators are released into a wilderness compound, where the brutal carnage commences. Combatants connive and, occasionally, cluster into groups but scrappy Katniss, a skilled archer, is determined to outwit and outlast the others while maintaining her integrity and humanity.

Collaboratively created by Suzanne Collins, Billy Ray and director Gary Ross (*Pleasantville, Seabiscuit*), it's an intense cautionary tale and visceral fable about ideological rebellions against totalitarianism. It's also an acerbic indictment of our voyeuristic obsession with reality television, like *Survivor.* What's also clear is that Panem's affluent citizens are desensitized to the Tributes' trauma and pain during the gruesome spectacle. But the obvious emotional undercurrents involving secondary characters aren't fully explored. Plus, it's bizarrely edited and too often photographed with a 'shaky cam,' like a docu-drama.

As gutsy, self-contained Katniss, Jennifer Lawrence (*Winter's Bone*) is compelling, smarmily supported by Stanley Tucci, Wes Bentley and Donald Sutherland.

On the Granger Movie Gauge of 1 to 10, *The Hunger Games* devours a humongous 9. It's tension-filled action-adventure, delivering a pulse-pounding, pop culture message of female empowerment.

The Illusionist (Sony Pictures Classics) (2010)

Earning a coveted Oscar nomination alongside *Toy Story 3* and *How to Train Your Dragon* for Best Animated Film is French director Sylvain Chomet's minimalist, melancholy homage to legendary French comic actor and filmmaker Jacques Tati, creator of *Mr. Hulot's Holiday* who died in 1982.

The wistful, almost wordless story revolves around an elderly vaudeville magician named Tatischeff (mumbled by Jean-Claude Donda) who packs up his recalcitrant rabbit, leaving Paris for London, where he realizes that rock 'n' roll has replaced his kind of sleight-of-hand act in the music halls. So this genteel, dignified performer winds up in Edinburgh, Scotland, where he attains modest success. Living in a shabby boarding house that's filled with circus performers, he befriends Alice (voiced by Eilidh Rankin), a naïve, young chambermaid who eventually becomes his assistant. Their evolving relationship is tender, paternal and touching, as generous Tatischeff takes on odd jobs to provide Alice with the luxuries she increasingly covets.

Adapted from a 1950s screenplay by Jacques Tati, entitled *Film Tati No. 4*, the script was inherited by Tati's late daughter, Sophie Tatischeff, who passed along the project to inventive Sylvain Chomet, best known for his 2003 Oscar-nominated *The Triplets of Belleville*.

Working in the Gothic quaintness of Edinburgh, Scotland, with his British wife and co-producer, Sally, writer/illustrator/composer/director Chomet conjures up a sweetly sad tone poem that's filled with bittersweet nostalgia, utilizing Walt Disney's archetypical, hand-drawn 2-D animation to create exquisite imagery, particularly shimmering reflections in department store windows. And in one remarkable scene, Chomet meticulously recreates *Mon Oncle*, one of Tati's classics. Since Jacques Tati was 6'3" tall, the magician's exaggerated frame is elongated, his hands are enlarged and his shoulders droop as he lurches forwards with Tati's familiarly uncertain gait.

A curious footnote concerns Tati's grandson, Richard Tatischeff Schiel McDonald, who told British news media that the idea sprang from his grandfather's guilt over abandoning his daughter, Helga Marie-Jeanne, who is McDonald's mother.

> On the Granger Movie Gauge of 1 to 10, *The Illusionist* is an enchanting 10—for 80 masterful minutes.

Inception (Warner Bros.) (2010)

Just as James Cameron fashioned a far-distant world in *Avatar*, Christopher Nolan has created an even more intriguing inner world in this terrifying new sci-fi thriller.

Dom Cobb (Leonardo DiCaprio) is a master of extraction. Trained in high-stakes corporate espionage and the use of psychotropic drugs, he steals thoughts that are buried deep in the subconscious when the mind is most vulnerable. Problem is: he's now an international fugitive, unable to return to his family in the United States. So when a wealthy, mysterious businessman (Ken Watanabe) offers him a way home, Cobb agrees to perform a far more dangerous feat: to implant an idea in the brain of an industrialist heir (Cillian Murphy).

Clever, always inventive writer/director Christopher Nolan (*The Dark Knight*, *Memento*) is fascinated by the relationship between waking life and dreaming particularly, as he says, by the fact that "everything within a dream – whether frightening or happy or fantastic – is being produced by your own mind, and what that says about the potential of the imagination is quite extraordinary."

As a result, Nolan's stylish, illusory dreamscapes defy the laws of time and physics, like an arresting Parisian cityscape folding in upon itself and an eye-popping chase sequence with weightless participants bouncing off walls in zero gravity. While revealing a dazzling myriad of mercurial perils that lurk in the subconscious, Nolan never violates the ingenious internal logic of his complex, sophisticated concept.

Delivering a multi-layered performance, Leonardo DiCaprio (*Shutter Island*) embodies a desperate man, haunted by secrets, with Joseph Gordon-Levitt (*500 Days of Summer*) as his trusted colleague, handling the high-tech details. Marion Cotillard (*La Vie en Rose*) is Cobb's late wife/the love of his life, and Ellen Page (*Juno*) is a brilliant architecture student who's intrigued by the opportunity to design and build interlocking, maze-like structures that don't exist in reality. Michael Caine, Tom Berenger, Pete Postlethwaite, Tom Hardy and Dileep Rao add pivotal support.

On the Granger Movie Gauge of 1 to 10, *Inception* is a tantalizing, tension-filled, mind-bending, time-twisting 10. It's the most exciting thrill-ride of the summer.

Indiana Jones and the Kingdom of the Crystal Skull (Paramount Pictures) (2008)

Indy's back! After nearly two decades, he dons his famous fedora, snaps his bullwhip and delivers punches that still pack enough of a wallop to clinch this summer's biggest blockbuster.

The fantasy-adventure begins in 1957 in the New Mexico desert, where Indy and his pal Mac (Ray Winstone) are pursued by villainous Soviet agents led by contemptuous parapsychologist Irina Spalko (Cate Blanchett).

After surviving an atomic bomb, Indy discovers he's lost his teaching position at Marshall College (filmed on the Yale campus in New Haven) because he's 'under government suspicion.' That's when he meets motorcycle-riding, switchblade-toting Mutt Williams (Shia LeBeouf, channeling Marlon Brando/James Dean), who carries a message imploring the adventurous archeologist to search for the legendary Crystal Skull of Akator, which the Russians also covet.

In the Peruvian jungle, along with the mysterious Mayan Skull, Indy finds his *Raiders of the Lost Ark* flame, irrepressible Marion Ravenwood (Karen Allen), whom he'd jilted at the altar. Plot-wise, that's all you need to know. Let the surprises unfold.

Conceived by George Lucas, written by David Koepp, directed by Steven Spielberg, and punctuated by John Williams' music, it's far-fetched, fast-paced fun. Middle-aged Harrison Ford is a bit mellower but he's still an intrepid, quick-with-a-quip leading man. All the stylistic Indy touches are there: the map with a moving red line indicating his travels and his inevitable encounter with a snake (a giant Olive Python), plus spectacular swordfights, ravenous red ants, subterranean caverns filled with gold, perilous plunges over waterfalls and lots of monkeys.

On the Granger Movie Gauge of 1 to 10, *Indiana Jones and the Kingdom of the Crystal Skull* is a terrific 10, an awesome, thrill-filled roller-coaster ride that you don't ever want to stop.

Inside Out (Pixar/Disney) (2015)

After a two-year hiatus, Pixar Animation (*The Incredibles, Wall-E, Toy Story*) is back with an incredibly creative, complex idea: how our various emotions affect our behavior.

The concept revolves around five instinctive emotions that propel us: Joy (Amy Poehler), Sadness (Phyllis Smith), Disgust (Mindy Kaling), Anger (Bill Hader) and Fear (Lewis Black). Headquartered in a vast Control Center in our mind, these emotions transfer experiences to vast memory banks, which is why —for example—we can remember pop jingles and silly songs.

When happy, playful eleven-year-old Riley (Kaitlyn Dias) is forced to move from her idyllic home in Minnesota to an old Victorian house in San Francisco, she has trouble adjusting. The three stabilities in her life – family, friendship and hockey – are shaken to the core.

While ebullient Joy dominated Riley's consciousness for many years, keeping wistful Sadness on the sidelines, now both Joy and Sadness are sucked from the Control Center and plunged into the countless, kaleidoscopic channels of her brain. That happens when Riley realizes she no longer has friends she can rely on and she loses confidence in her ability to play hockey.

Director Pete Docter (*Up*) explores "inside" Riley's mind, which reacts to the "outside" world. Sounds confusing? It isn't. Particularly at the dinner table when Mom (Diane Lane) and Dad (Kyle MacLachlan) react to a very petulant, pre-teen Riley's moody rebellion, which is a reflection of her insecurity.

Pixar animators visualize the inner workings of the brain and simplify them—with honesty, subtle humor and compassion to spare. Each experience is depicted as a marble, which rolls through a series of ramps and chutes, landing on a Train-of-Thought, perhaps bypassing Long Term Memory, leading to Abstract Thinking, even Goofball Island.

There's even a dazzling, surreal dream sequence with Riley's imaginary childhood friend Bing Bong (Richard Kind), evoking memories of Walt Disney's *Fantasia*. The result is colorful, captivating and funny, illustrating a universal experience that engages both kids and adults.

On the Granger Movie Gauge of 1 to 10, *Inside Out* is a terrific, triumphant 10, emerging as one of the most ambitious, exciting animated features ever made. And watch the closing credits.

The Insider (Buena Vista Pictures) (1999)

Michael Mann's compelling story, adapted by Mann and Eric Roth from Marie Brenner's 1996 *Vanity Fair* article, "The Man Who Knew Too Much," examines the behind-the-scenes drama and maneuverings that led to the media's exposure of tobacco industry fraud.

Whistle-blower Jeffrey Wigand, former head of research and development at Brown & Williamson, was a corporate officer, the ultimate insider on the skullduggery involved in the business of selling tobacco. His firing comes to the attention of Mike Wallace's producer, Lowell Bergman, who convinces the reluctant scientist to spill the beans on "60 Minutes", only to have the interview killed by CBS's corporate lawyer who cites a confidentiality agreement the executive signed with the tobacco company. Three months later, after the *Wall Street Journal* printed Wigand's allegations, "60 Minutes" aired the segment. So much for fiasco.

It's the Oscar-caliber performances that command attention, primarily the emotional relationship between Russell Crowe, as the conflicted Wigand, and Al Pacino, as the tenacious Bergman. A journalist hasn't shown this much righteous indignation since "All the President's Men."

Christopher Plummer deserves a Best Supporting Actor nod as Wallace, who with Philip Baker Hall, as producer Don Hewitt, come across as cowards, bowing to management on ethics, leaving their source, Wigand, hanging in the wind. The medieval and Middle Eastern music by Lisa Gerrard and Pieter Bourke enhances Dante Spinotti's dark, eerie imagery.

On the Granger Movie Gauge of 1 to 10, *The Insider* is a tense, trenchantly topical 10. Subsequent to the shocking events dramatized in the film, the tobacco industry settled the lawsuits filed against it by Mississippi and 49 other states for $246 billion.

It Happened One Night
(Columbia Pictures) (1934)

This 1934 romantic comedy, directed by Frank Capra, was the first picture to win all five major Academy Awards (Best Picture, Director, Actress, Actor and Screenplay), a feat not matched again until *One Flew Over the Cuckoo's Nest* (1975) and *The Silence of the Lambs* (1991).

Based on Samuel Hopkins Adams' short story, *Night Bus*, adapted by Robert Riskin, the plot revolves around Ellen "Ellie" Andrews (Claudette Colbert), a spoiled socialite who defies her wealthy, influential father, Alexander Andrews (Walter Connolly), by marrying fortune-hunter "King" Westley (Jameson Thomas). When her father annuls the marriage, Ellie bolts, boarding a bus from Miami to New York City. En route, she meets a roguish newspaper reporter, Peter Warne (Clark Gable), who recognizes her and gives her a choice: either she'll give him an "exclusive" story in return for his help in finding Westley - or - he'll call her father and collect the reward offered for her return. A series of screwball misadventures then ensues.

Curiously, neither star was the original choice. The part of Ellie was offered to Miriam Hopkins, Myrna Loy, Margaret Sullavan, Constance Bennett, Bette Davis, Loretta Young and Carole Lombard before Claudette Colbert. She'd had an unpleasant experience working with Frank Capra in her first film, "For the Love of Mike," and demanded that her salary be doubled to $50,000 and her commitment limited to four weeks of filming. Reportedly, M.G.M.'s chief Louis B. Mayer lent Clark Gable to Columbia Pictures, known then as Poverty Row, over his strenuous objections after Robert Montgomery turned down the reporter role. Working together, Colbert and Gable developed a sense of camaraderie. And after accepting her "unexpected" Oscar, Colbert publicly thanked Capra for making the film which she'd predicted to be "the worst picture in the world."

In December, 1996, Steven Spielberg bought Gable's Oscar at auction for $607,000 and donated it to the Motion Picture Academy. The following year, Colbert's Oscar was offered at auction by Christie's; no bids were made for it. This film not only ignited nationwide interest in traveling by Greyhound bus but also torpedoed the undershirt industry because, when Gable removed his shirt, he was bare-chested.

India's Bollywood has successfully remade it twice as *Chori Chori*, starring Raj Kapoor and Nargis, and *Dil Hai Ki Manta Nahin*, starring Aamir Khan and Pooja Bhatt.

On the Granger Movie Gauge of 1 to 10, *It Happened One Night* is a pivotal 10, marking Frank Capra's creation of the screwball comedy genre, characterized by escapism, farce, fast-paced repartee and conflicting socio-economic classes.

It's a Wonderful Life (RKO Radio) (1946)

Jimmy Stewart was never a particularly ambitious actor, never wanted to direct or form his own production company. Indeed, after returning home from W.W. II service, he considered leaving Hollywood. Lionel Barrymore talked him out of it, telling him: "Don't ever forget that acting is the greatest profession ever invented. When you act, you move millions of people, shape their lives, give them a sense of exaltation. No other profession has that power."

Jimmy Stewart loved this movie; it was his favorite: "(Director) Frank Capra called me one day and said he had an idea for a picture, inspired from a Christmas card that somebody sent him. There was a verse on it saying, in effect, that everybody was born for some purpose and that the world would be a sadder place if they had not lived."

In Bedford Falls, New York, on Christmas Eve, George Bailey (Stewart) is despondent. All his life he'd wanted to leave "this crummy little town," explore the world and do big things. Contemplating suicide, he's confronted by his guardian angel, Clarence Odbody (Henry Travers), who gives him a chance to see what his community would have been like without him. Based on historian/novelist Philip Van Doren Stern's short story, "The Greatest Gift," it was adapted by Frances Goodrich, Albert Hackett, Jo Swerling and director Frank Capra, who cast Donna Reed as Bailey's wife—with a strong supporting cast of character actors including Lionel Barrymore, Frank Faylen, Tommy Mitchell, H.B. Warner and Ward Bond.

To replicate falling snow, Hollywood had always used cornflakes painted white. But they were noisy, obliterating dialogue, so a new effect was developed using a fire-fighting chemical, foamite, with soap and water. This mixture was pumped at high pressure through a wind-machine to create silent, falling snow. For this, RKO Effects department received a special technical award from the Academy.

This 1946 supernatural drama received five Academy nominations but won no Oscars. After an initially disappointing box-office, its popularity grew, particularly after its copyright expired due to a clerical error and it was shown repeatedly on American television, especially during the Christmas season. The original musical ending was "Ode to Joy," not "Auld Lang Syne." Seneca Falls, New York, maintains it was Capra's model for Bedford Falls and hosts an annual "It's a Wonderful Life" festival with Hotel Clarence named after the guardian angel.

On the Granger Movie Gauge of 1 to 10, *It's a Wonderful Life* is an inspirational 10, a spiritual masterpiece.

Journey to the Center of the Earth (20th Century Fox) (1959)

Inspired by Jules Verne's novel, this 1959 CinemaScope sci-fi fantasy has courageous characters, intimidating villains and scary monsters.

The story begins in 1880 in Edinburgh, Scotland, where recently-knighted geology professor Oliver Lindenbrook (James Mason) is given a curious volcanic rock paperweight by Alec McKuen (Pat Boone), one of his students. When Lindenbrook melts its lava covering, the rock explodes, revealing a plumb-bob (a metal weight that hangs from a string, used to calibrate a straight vertical line in surveying) with an etched message from long-lost Icelandic explorer Arne Saknussem, who—300 years earlier—disappeared into an extinct volcano while searching for the center of the Earth.

That precipitates a race between intrepid Lindenbrook and his sneaky scientific rival, Stockholm Professor Goteborg (Ivan Triesault), who captures and imprisons Lindenbrook and McKuen. After they're freed by husky Hans Bjelke (Peter Ronson) with his pet duck Gertrude, they discover that Goteborg has been poisoned. His widow, Carla (Arlene Dahl), offers her husband's equipment, including valuable Ruhmkorff lamps, but only on the condition that she accompany them on their wondrous expedition. What they don't realize is that they're being followed by evil Count Saknussem (Thayer David), a descendant of the original explorer.

Scripted by Charles Brackett (best known for his collaborations with writer/director Billy Wilder on *Ninotchka* and *Sunset Boulevard*) and directed by Henry Levin, it's like taking a fanciful amusement-park ride, encountering luminescent algae, a subterranean ocean, the lost city of Atlantis, a forest of giant mushrooms, prehistoric Dimetrodons and a giant scorpion—- accompanied by Bernard Hermann's excellent score. This is the first and it remains the best version of Verne's classic story.

James Mason replaced an ailing Clifton Webb as Professor Lindenbrook before filming began. And, reportedly, Pat Boone was talked into taking this part by his agent. Years later, he said he's glad he did—not only because of the regular residual checks but also because it's the movie he'll probably be best remembered for.

It was nominated for three Academy Awards: Best Art Direction/Set Decoration, Best Special Effects and Best Sound—and, despite the dated technology, it's still lots of fun to watch.

On the Granger Movie Gauge of 1 to 10, *Journey to the Center of the Earth* is a whimsical, escapist 8, a lighthearted, family-friendly adventure that stands the test of time

The King's Speech
(Weinstein Company) (2010)

Colin Firth is extraordinary and Geoffrey Rush is electrifying in this engrossing, fact-based historical drama, set in England during the 1930s.

Shy, uptight Albert (Firth), Duke of York, is second in the line of succession after his reckless, flamboyant older brother, Prince Edward (Guy Pearce). That's fine with him because his lifelong struggle with a paralyzing stammer makes giving a speech nearly impossible, causing members of the dysfunctional Royal family to be abusive. But when Edward abdicates (becoming Duke of Windsor) in order to marry Wallis Simpson (Eve Best), a twice-divorced American, Albert is forced to prepare for his Coronation— with Hitler's invasion of Europe looming on the horizon. Radio has revolutionized how people perceive their monarch so it's imperative that the future King—soon to be known as George VI, father of Queen Elizabeth II—be able to communicate in order to lead Britain, along with Winston Churchill (Timothy Spall), into World War II.

Encouraged by his wife Elizabeth (Helena Bonham-Carter), Prince Albert reluctantly engages the services of an eccentric, dubiously credentialed speech therapist and frustrated Australian actor named Lionel Logue (Geoffrey Rush), who impertinently insists on calling his client by his first name – "Bertie" – rather than the customary "Your Majesty." Their unlikely, completely unconventional relationship forms the emotional crux of the story as, gradually, Albert gains confidence in his voice and learns to cope with his crippling impediment.

For his poignant performance, Colin Firth is front-runner for the Best Actor Oscar. Geoffrey Rush should be first-in-line as Best Supporting Actor with Helena Bonham-Carter scoring as Best Supporting Actress. Expect literate screenwriter David Seidler and deft director Tom Hooper also to deservedly garner Oscar nominations. And Seidler's Broadway adaptation is set to open next spring.

On the Granger Movie Gauge of 1 to10, *The King's Speech* is a superlative 10, definitely one of the 10 Best of 2010. Since stuttering affects more than three million Americans, sufferers from this complex disorder are urged to contact The Stuttering Foundation http://www.stutteringhelp.org/ effective treatments are now available.

The Kite Runner (Paramount Classics/ Vantage) (2007)

Marc Forster's timely adaptation of Khaled Hosseini's bestseller about the doomed friendship of two Afghan boys is not only faithful to the book but enhances the narrative with resonant visuals.

The sprawling, generation-spanning epic begins in 1978 in Kabul, Afghanistan, where timid, twelve-year-old Amir (Zekiria Ebrahimi), who lives with his aristocratic widower father (Homayoun Ershadi), loves playing with his best friend, Hassan (Ahmad Khan Mahmoodzada), the spunky son of their servant. Since Amir is literate, he often reads aloud to Hassan under a pomegranate tree, but—most of all—they excel at kite-flying competition. But one fateful day, Amir cowardly betrays Hassan, who is then sexually brutalized by older bullies. After that, Amir's shame drives a wedge between them—and their country is torn asunder by the Soviet invasion.

Years later, married and living in San Francisco, now-grown Amir (Khalid Abdalla) receives a phone call from an old family friend, informing him that Hassan is dead, leaving a young son orphaned. Guilt-ridden, Amir embarks on a dangerous journey to his ravaged homeland to find and rescue the boy (Ali Dinesh) and bring him to California. Traveling in disguise in treacherous Taliban territory, Amir must cover his shaven face with a false beard and witness a sharia, the public ritual stoning of an adulterous couple.

The non-professional children, discovered in local Kabul schools by casting director Kate Dowd, are extraordinary, and the Middle Eastern actors acquit themselves impressively. Using subtitles, screenwriter David Benioff has, by necessity, condensed the complexity while retaining the ethnic/culture-clash drama, and Roberto Schaefer's lyrical cinematography deftly uses China doubling for Afghanistan.

On the Granger Movie Gauge of 1 to 10, *The Kite Runner* soars to an exceptional, enthralling 10—with its universal themes of honor and redemption.

Kon-Tiki (The Weinstein Company) (2012)

Back in 1947, Norwegian explorer Thor Hyerdahl decided to cross 4,300 miles of Pacific Ocean on a huge balsa-wood raft called Kon-Tiki, named for the Polynesian sun god. Heyerdahl was determined to prove that, about 1,500 years ago, South Americans crossed the sea and settled in the South Pacific. His book about that perilous expedition has sold more than 50 million copies and has been translated in close to 70 languages. His cinematic chronicle won the Best Documentary Oscar in 1950.

Norwegian actor Pal Sverre Hagen plays charismatic Thor Heyerdahl, whose blond/blue-eyed physicality is reminiscent of Peter O'Toole in "Lawrence of Arabia." Financed by the Peruvian government, Heyerdahl and his brave crew of five men—four Norwegians and a Swede - spent more than 100 days afloat, encountering whales and sharks, along with treacherous storms, as a radio operator did his best to stay in contact—when the transmitter worked. While he did bring along a movie camera, Heyerdahl had no motor onboard and was resolute about building his raft using only the indigenous materials available to the original sailors, insisting that logs be lashed together with rope, not wire, despite the pleadings of one of his crew.

The Norwegian version of this new bio pic was nominated for this year's Best Foreign Language Film but lost to Michael Haneke's *Amour*. Now, an English-language version is playing in local theaters.

Directors Joachim Ronning and Espen Sandberg filmed in both languages simultaneously to appeal to the international market, utilizing a script written by Petter Skavlan. Each scene was shot first in Norwegian, then in English. Many years ago, when Hollywood first introduced sound, multiple language versions were more common than they are today. By the mid-1930s, however, dubbing and subtitles took over. In recent years, the most commercially viable dual-language film was Angelina Jolie's Serbo-Croatian/English *In the Land of Blood in Honey*, set in Sarajevo during the Bosian War of the 1990s.

On the Granger Movie Gauge of 1 to 10, *Kon-Tiki* is an astonishing, adventurous 8. And there's more to come...directors Joachim Renning and Espen Sandberg just signed with Disney to helm the forthcoming fifth *Pirates of the Caribbean* installment with Johnny Depp.

Labyrinth of Lies
(Sony Pictures Classics) (2014)

In Germany after World War II, when reconstruction and the Federal Republic took over, the majority of the population tried to forget the atrocities of Hitler's Third Reich. That led to a postwar generation that either never heard of Auschwitz or dismissed it as American propaganda.

So in 1958, when Johann Radmann (Alexander Fehling) becomes a junior prosecutor in Frankfurt, he's intrigued when an investigative journalist, Thomas Gnielka (Andre Szymanski) reports that an artist, Simon Kirsch (Johannes Krisch), recognized a schoolteacher as the former SS guard who brutalized him.

Naïve Radmann immediately encounters resistance to his inquiries. Prosecutor General Fritz Bauer (Gert Voss) says that it's a lost cause because he'll need proof of murder, since all other war crimes expired under the statute of limitations, adding that the entire German civil service is filled with former Nazis.

Nevertheless, with Gnielka's help, Radmann launches an investigation encompassing 8,000 people who worked at Auschwitz. The odds are daunting as Radmann views the U.S. Army Document Center archives in Wiesbaden, where records of 600,000 suspects are haphazardly stored.

Driven by shame and guilt, along with societal complicity involving his own family, Radmann becomes obsessive in his arduous research. Eventually, 22 former Nazis were tried for murder, none of whom were repentant or apologetic.

Unlike the famous Nuremburg trials in the 1940s by the Allies against surviving members of the Nazi high command, the Auschwitz trials (1963-1965) were prosecuted by Germans themselves against fellow countrymen.

Italian-born German director Giulio Ricciarelli and co-writer Elizabeth Bartel created Radmann as a composite of three real-life German prosecutors. He's the young idealist battling an entrenched bureaucracy. And they wisely resisted the temptation to utilize familiar concentration camp footage when Radmann eventually visits Poland.

There's also a romantic subplot involving an enterprising young dressmaker (Friederike Becht) whom Radmann initially prosecuted in traffic court. And an attempt to capture elusive Dr. Josef Mengele.

On the Granger Movie Gauge of 1 to 10, *Labyrinth of Lies* is an engrossing, enlightening 8. It's Germany's Academy Award submission as Best Foreign Language Film.

Les Miserables (Universal Pictures) (2012)

Based on Victor Hugo's classic 1862 novel, this epic, cinematic adaptation should attract audiences that have loved the Broadway musical over the years.

Set in squalid 19th century France, the film opens in 1815 with emaciated Jean Valjean (Hugh Jackman) as prisoner 24601, serving 19 years at hard labor for stealing of a loaf of bread, under the watchful eye of implacable Inspector Javert (Russell Crowe). Eventually paroled, Valjean is condemned as an unemployable ex-convict.

The sympathetic Bishop of Digne (Colm Wilkinson, who originally played Valjean on Broadway) gives him food and shelter; in return, Valjean steals the Church's silver candlesticks. When Valjean is caught, the Bishop tells the authorities that the booty belongs to Valjean, instructing Valjean to use it to make a better life. Within eight years, Valjean becomes a wealthy factory owner, known as Monsieur Madeleine.

He takes pity on single mother-turned-prostitute, Fantine (Anne Hathaway), desperately protecting her daughter, Cosette, by paying disreputable innkeepers (Helena Bonham Carter, Sacha Baron Cohen). Years later, with brawny Valjean as her protective guardian/adoptive father, now-grown Cosette (Amanda Seifried) falls in love with rebellious Marius (Eddie Redmayne) during the 1832 Paris Uprising.

Written by William Nicholson, Alain Boublil, Claude-Michel Schoenberg and Herbert Kretzmer, it's bombastically directed by Tom Hooper (*The King's Speech*), who retains the pop opera structure with only minimal spoken dialogue. Hooper's innovation is having the actors sing 'live' on the set, as opposed to recording with an orchestra beforehand; this was done only once before, unsuccessfully, by Peter Bogdanovich in the disastrous At Long Last Love (1975).

Exuding agony, Hugh Jackman nails Valjean's "Soliloquy," "Bring Him Home" and "Who Am I?" with every emotion magnified by close-ups. Anne Hathaway's "I Dreamed a Dream" is wrenching, assuring her major Oscar contention, echoed by Samantha Barks' plaintive "On My Own." Russell Crowe tentatively warbles "Stars," while Helena Bonham Carter and Sacha Baron Cohen romp through "Master of the House."

On the Granger Movie Gauge of 1 to 10, *Les Miserables* is an anguished, unrestrained, relentlessly amplified 9, a uniquely overwhelming, even exhausting extravaganza.

Let the Right One In (Magnolia Pictures/ Magnet Releasing) (2008)

Set in a wintry Stockholm suburb, this vampire/horror love story gives a tender, unique twist to the bloodsucking thriller genre that dates back to the classic 1922 *Nosferatu*.

Thin, pale, introverted Oskar (Kare Hedebrant) is relentlessly tormented by bigger classmates, so the shy twelve-year-old generally keeps to himself, concocting elaborate revenge fantasies. But then, one evening, he meets sad-eyed, dark-haired Eli (Lina Leandersson), also 12, who has just moved into an adjacent apartment with a man who is presumably her father (Per Ragnar).

About the same time, there are a series of gruesome murders. A man is found hanging upside down in a tree in the park, his blood draining out; another corpse is frozen in the lake; and a woman is bitten on the neck. Noticing that Eli only ventures out in the dark shadows of night and never seems to cringe in the cold, Oskar catches on to her grisly secret rather quickly, yet he's determined to make her his girlfriend. Their relationship grows rather than diminishes, although the emotionally conflicted Eli cautions, "I cannot be your friend."

Nevertheless, the two adolescents soon become inseparable so, when school bullies return to torment Oskar, who seems unable to fight back, Eli defends him the only way she can. Based on the best-selling novel by John Ajvide Lindqvist, Swedish filmmaker Tomas Alfredson creates an enthralling, subtly disturbing story by astutely casting youthful newcomers Kare Hedebrant and Lina Leanandersson, who are totally convincing in their respective roles, and trusting the creepy, atmospheric cinematography of Hoyte Van Hoytema to generate a pervasive aura of tragic dread.

On the Granger Movie Gauge of 1 to 10, *Let the Right One In* is a chilling 10, a haunting, suspenseful coming-of-age tale.

Letters from Iwo Jima
(Warner Bros.) (2006)

Clint Eastwood's back-to-back *Flags of Our Fathers* and *Letters from Iwo Jima* are unique in that they present the same devastating W.W. II battle – but from different perspectives.

While the Americans eventually prevailed on Iwo Jima, the 20,000 Japanese troops there, faced with certain death, put up a heroic fight for 40 days although they were outnumbered five-to-one. Under the cunning leadership of Lt. Gen. Tadamichi Kuribayashi (Ken Watanabe of "The Last Samurai"), who had traveled and studied in America, they dug 18 miles of labyrinthine tunnels in Mt. Suribachi.

While his men were prepared to "die with honor" to defend the tiny, volcanic island they considered part of Japan's sacred homeland, Kuribayashi told them that each had to kill 10 enemy soldiers before they did, specifically American "medics." One of his bravest cohorts is bon vivant equestrian Baron Nishi (Tsuyoshi Ihara), who rode in the 1932 Olympics in Los Angeles. Noble, compassionate and aware of their hopeless task, both are reluctant victims of Japanese militarism.

Screenwriter Iris Yamashita worked with Paul Haggis (*Million Dollar Baby*), inspired by a collection of letters by Kuribayashi to his wife, daughter and son, published in Japan, as well as from hundreds of servicemen's letters that were excavated decades later.

Often read aloud, these letters introduce insightful flashbacks into the personal lives of the Imperial Army's conscripted combatants, like Saigo (pop star Kazurani Ninomiya), a baker yearning for his wife and infant daughter; idealistic Shimizu (Ryo Kase); and suicidal Ito (Shidou Nakamura) who refuses to surrender.

In Japanese with English subtitles, *Letters from Iwo Jima* is an extraordinary, resonant 10. Subtle and non-judgmental, *Flags of Our Fathers* and *Letters from Iwo Jima* examine history within its context and emerge as strikingly effective anti-war statements.

Life of Pi (Fox 2000) (2012)

Adapting Yann Martel's acclaimed novel for the screen was a daunting challenge, one that Oscar-winning director Ang Lee tackled with inspired imagination. This exquisitely enchanting, emotionally engaging, spiritual fantasy begins and ends in Montreal, where a writer (Rafe Spall) is interviewing middle-aged Picine Militor Patel (Irrfan Khan), who relates the incredible adventure of his life as a thoughtful meditation on God.

Named after a Parisian swimming pool, curious Picine, known as Pi, grew up as Hindu/Catholic in Pondicherry, a former French colony in southern India, where his father (Adil Hussain) ran a zoo. Forced by economic stress, the family plans to move their menagerie to Canada. But when their Japanese cargo ship sinks in a terrifying storm, teenage Pi (Suraj Sharma) is stranded on a lifeboat with a wounded zebra, an orange orangutan, a manic hyena and a ferocious Bengal tiger, named Richard Parker. For 227 days, he manages to survive, adrift in the middle of the Pacific Ocean, courageously coping with grief, faith and that ravenous tiger.

Working from a sensitive, lyrical screenplay by David Magee (*Finding Neverland*), who effectively adapts the symbolic, Robinson Crusoe-like, coming-of-age fable, Ang Lee filmed in India and Taiwan, where a huge water tank was constructed in the central city of Taichung. His primary problem was coping with the animals on a churning sea and he credits cutting-edge 3-D technology for achieving the vividly striking, visually stunning effects he wanted - with David Gropman's elegant production design and Mychael Danna's evocative score.

Known for his versatility, Ang Lee's credits include *Brokeback Mountain, Crouching Tiger, Hidden Dragon, The Ice Storm, Hulk* and *Sense and Sensibility*. Here, Lee and cinematographer Claudio Miranda capture with impeccable craftsmanship, Pi's engaging encounters with Richard Parker, flying fish, luminous sea creatures and a surreal, carnivorous island populated by meerkats.

On the Granger Movie Gauge of 1 to 10, *Life of Pi* is an awesome, astounding 10. It's not only one of the best pictures of the year but also must be seen in 3-D on as big a screen as possible.

Lincoln (DreamWorks) (2012)

Back in 1863, President Abraham Lincoln proclaimed Thanksgiving a national holiday. That's not part of Steven Spielberg's epic historical drama but adds to the timeliness of its release.

Opening with scenes of Civil War carnage, reminiscent of *Saving Private Ryan*, this is a cinematic chronicle of the last months in the life of the 16th President of the United States. Based partly on Doris Kearns Goodwin's *Team of Rivals: The Political Genius of Abraham Lincoln,* Tony Kushner's sensitive, compelling script concentrates on Lincoln's determination to unite our divided nation and to convince rowdy, cantankerous curmudgeons in the House of Representatives of the necessity of passing the 13th Amendment to the Constitution which would permanently abolish slavery. Willing to offer bribery and patronage, Lincoln was a shrewd genius of complicated political strategy.

In the title role, Daniel Day-Lewis is conflicted yet canny and commanding. Not only is the physical resemblance convincing, including the stooped posture, but Day-Lewis also alters his normal baritone to speak in a lighter, warmer tenor voice, appropriate for the witty quips and folksy storytelling of an engaging raconteur. Authoritative and paternal, this is the finest performance you will see all year, equal to and, perhaps, surpassing his Oscar-winning *My Left Foot* and *There Will Be Blood.*

Steven Spielberg's casting choices are impeccable. Sally Field and Tommy Lee Jones embody distraught Mary Todd Lincoln and crusading Congressman Thaddeus Stevens, respectively. Memorable in the ensemble are David Strathairn, Hal Holbrook, John Hawkes, Joseph Gordon-Levitt and James Spader.

The production values are impressive, particularly Spielberg's subtle use of chiaroscuro lighting, adding to period authenticity. He introduces Mary Todd Lincoln as seen through a mirror, indicating the emotional divide between her and her husband. And that's just one of his astute directorial touches. The rest of his technical team includes cinematographer Janusz Kaminski, film editor Michael Kahn and composer John Williams.

On the Granger Movie Gauge of 1 to 10, *Lincoln* is a superlative, spellbinding 10. This surprisingly relevant observation on the essence of leadership is, undoubtedly, one of the best pictures of the year.

The Lives of Others (Sony Pictures Classics) (2006)

Deservedly, this is Oscar's Best Foreign Film. Set in the mid-1980s in the German Democratic Republic before the fall of the Berlin Wall, it's writer/director Florian Henckel von Donnersmarck's haunting tale of obsessive voyeurism.

Gerd Weisler (Ulriche Muhe) is a captain in the Stasi, the Communitists' secret police. He's told by his superior (Ulrich Tukur) to install surveillance on Georg Dreyman (Sebastian Koch), a celebrated but controversial playwright who lives with charismatic actress Christa-Maria Sieland (Martina Gedeck). From his attic perch, Gerd becomes addicted to watching their lives unfold, his own 'live' soap opera. Gradually, Gerd's drab, solitary existence is significantly changed by what he learns about love, relationships, corruption, power, deception and betrayal, and a metamorphosis takes place. Eventually, he hides incriminating evidence and falsifies official records.

What emerges is a Cold War political thriller, revolving around surveillance and the state's control of people's lives – that's also an intensely human drama. The script is subtle, the cast superb. But it's von Donnersmarck's deft, atmospheric direction that creates the intense claustrophobia.

"Over the years, there were several things that led me to make this film," he says. "As a young boy, I found it interesting and exciting to feel the fear of adults during our visits to East Berlin. My parents were afraid when they crossed the border. And our friends from East Germany were afraid when others saw that they were speaking with us. Then I had this image of a man sitting in a bleak room, wearing headphones and listening to beautiful music even though he didn't want to hear it."

On the Granger Movie Gauge of 1 to 10, *The Lives of Others* is an unforgettable 10, the most electrifying German film in more than a decade.

Lord of the Rings: Return of the King (New Line Cinema) (2003)

New Zealand director Peter Jackson's final chapter is the best of his Middle Earth trilogy, based on J.R.R. Tolkien's classic sci-fi/fantasy - and the film to beat at this year's Oscars!

The 3 1/2-hour epic begins where *The Two Towers* ended. While the naive, innocent hobbits, Frodo Baggins (Elijah Wood) and his loyal pal Sam Gamgee (Sean Astin), are trudging with The Ring toward Mount Doom in Mordor, led by the treacherous Gollum (a CGI-creation, voiced by Andy Serkis), their cohorts are preparing for a great battle against the fearsome, evil legions of Sauron, led by the Orcs with their colossal Oliphaunts and reptilian Fell Beasts. Valiant Aragorn (Viggo Mortensen), the Elf archer Legolas (Orlando Bloom) and the Dwarf Gimli (John Rhys-Davies) join with the Wizard Gandalf (Ian McKellen) to defend Gondor's city of Minis Tirith.

Arwen (Liv Tyler) and Galadriel (Cate Blanchett) exert their ethereal influence, yet Frodo must face the peril of the giant spider Shelob, as Aragon enlists the aid of the ephemeral Army of the Dead, and Eowyn of Rohan (Miranda Otto) becomes a mighty warrior.

Cleverly, Jackson and his co-writers (Fran Walsh, Philippa Boyens) build up an intimate, emotional attachment to these characters, vividly developing their rivalries and relationships, even revealing the Gollum's backstory, amid the tumultuous action. Grant Major's ingenious production design and Andrew Lesnie's cinematography are spectacular.

Despite the fact that it's at least 1/2 hour too long, on the Granger Movie Gauge of 1 to 10, *Lord of the Rings: Return of the King* is a towering, transcendental 10. It's an enormously exciting, exquisite, even exhausting, cinematic experience. Definitely one of the 10 BEST MOVIES of 2003.

Lore (Music Box Films) (2012)

Set in 1945 in the Bavarian countryside just after Germany has surrendered near the end of W.W. II, this is the coming-of-age/survival story of teenage Hannalore Dressler (Saskia Rosendahl), nicknamed Lore, who is left in charge when her parents are taken into custody for war crimes during the Third Reich. Just before her mother (Ursina Lardi) departs, she instructs stolid, responsible Lore to take her four younger siblings—ranging in age from an infant to pre-teen—to their grandmother's house, some 500 miles to the north, near Hamburg.

As they traipse across the Black Forest countryside, where bloodied corpses lie unburied, they barter their meager possessions for food and medicine. Anti-Semitism is rampant, as many villagers believe that the shameful Holocaust images posted on bulletin boards were staged by actors. Along the way, they're stopped by American soldiers who demand to see their identification papers.

Observing their fearful dilemma is Thomas (Kai Malina), a German lad with a number tattooed on his arm; he is pretending to be a Jew in an attempt to avoid incarceration by the Allies. Coming to their rescue with his stolen papers containing a yellow star, he says they're his siblings, traveling from Buchenwald to Auschwitz before liberation. While grateful, sullen Lore is, nevertheless, stubbornly conflicted; her Nazi indoctrination through Hitler's Youth Corps has taught her to distrust and loathe Jews. As their journey is fraught with danger, Thomas becomes their leader and guardian, arousing Lore's sexuality and forcing her to question her beliefs.

Spoken entirely in German and directed with stunning detachment and admirable restraint, it's helmed by Australian director Cate Shortland, who adapted Robin Mukherjee's screenplay, based on one of three stories in Rachel Seiffert's 2001 novel *The Dark Room*. Selected as Australia's entry for the Best Foreign Language Oscar at the 85th Academy Awards, it didn't make the final shortlist.

On the Granger Movie Gauge of 1 to 10, *Lore* is an indelible 9, truthfully chronicling the triumph of the human spirit and in a class with Michael Haneke's *The White Ribbon*.

Mad Max: Fury Road
(Warner Bros.) (2015)

Wow! Director/writer/producer George Miller's post-apocalyptic action adventure is a blast!

While wearily haunted ex-cop Max Rockatansky (Tom Hardy) is the titular hero, hunted in the toxic, dystopian Wasteland, Charlize Theron delivers a powerhouse performance as Imperator Furiosa, the most exciting sci-fi protagonist since Ellen Ripley (*Alien*). As George Miller explains, "What looks like testosterone-fueled summer escape is actually a badass feminist action flick. The men do the damage but the women restore humanity."

Furiosa is a War Rig operator who's determined to wreak revenge for her past suffering by smuggling the prized Five Wives (Rosie Huntington-Whiteley, Riley Keogh, Zoe Kravitz, Abbey Lee, Courtney Eaton) of the tyrannical warlord, Immortan Joe (Hugh Keays-Byrne), to safety in the Green Place.

They've been enslaved in the Citadel to breed and provide breast milk to the white-painted, tattooed troops, a.k.a. War Boys (including Nicolas Hoult), who dream of an idyllic afterlife in Valhalla. Since both Max and Furiosa are pursued by Immortan Joe and his crazed son, Corpus Colossus (Quentin Kenihan), they reluctantly team up for mutual survival, battling the Gas Town thugs and Bullet Farmer gang, along with the underground Buzzard tribe and the stealthy Rock Riders.

British actor Tom Hardy (*The Dark Knight Rises, Locke*) and Charlize Theron (Oscar-winner for *Monster* and *Prometheus*) are dynamite together, wreaking spectacular vehicular vengeance.

Back in 1979, George Miller created iconic Mad Max, catapulting Mel Gibson to stardom as the righteous, leather-jacketed nomad. But its allegorical antecedents go back to classic Greek mythology (*Odysseus*), Westerns (*The Man with No Name*), even *Star Wars* Han Solo. "One of the ideas that drove [the original] *Mad Max*, and [also] drives *Fury Road*, was Alfred Hitchcock's notion about making films that can be watched anywhere in the world without subtitles," Miller says, explaining how his production team used music to viscerally propel the plot. Miller also recruited playwright Eve Ensler (*Vagina Diaries*) to authenticate the depiction of vulnerable, abused women.

FYI: With her bright red hair, it's easy to spot Riley Keogh, who is Elvis Presley's granddaughter.

On the Granger Movie Gauge of 1 to 10, *Mad Max: Fury Road* is an assaultive, intense 8, delivering an outrageously relentless adrenaline rush.

A Man and a Woman (Allied Artists) (1966)

It's probably fair to say that this romantic drama, released in the summer of 1966, was the first to entice many Americans to see a subtitled French film. After winning the Palme d'Or at the Cannes Film Festival, it won two Academy Awards: Best Screenplay and Best Foreign Film.

A man, Jean-Louis Duroc (Jean-Louis Trintignant), and a woman, Anne Gauthier (Anouk Aime), both widowed, meet while visiting their respective children at a boarding school in Deauville. Returning home, she misses her train, so he offers to drive her back to Paris. She tells him that she is a film script supervisor and her late husband Pierre (Pierre Borough) was a movie stuntman who was killed while making a film. Jean-Louis and Anne meet again the following Sunday and take her daughter Francois (Souad Amidou) and his son Antoine (Antoine Sire) to lunch.

Driving back that night, he tells her about his life as a racing-car driver, how he was almost killed in a crash and how his distraught wife Valerie (Valerie Lagrange) committed suicide. Despite various psychological impediments, their erratic romance evolves.

Writer/director/cinematographer/producer Claude Lelouch noted: "The subject—passion against marriage, life against death, speed against love. It is a film of emotions. The sound was more important than the words, the colors more enchanting than the scenery. Every moment was a cry, the sound of a car engine, a song…. with this film, I became convinced that one must not narrate but express. What the characters did not say was often more important that what they said."

Lelouch was a pioneer in mixing different film stocks: black-and-white with sepia and color, 35 mm with 16 mm and super 8. Throughout the film, Francis Lai's highly melodic score, which was recorded prior to filming, blends with the narrative, reflecting Lelouch's training doing short films for Scopitones, juke boxes equipped with small motion-picture screens that served as forerunners of music videos. In Finland, Lai's theme song is instantly recognizable since it's used by the Silja Line cruise ferry. And Lai later went on to create the indelible theme music for *Love Story*.

> On the Granger Movie Gauge of 1 to 10, *A Man and a Woman* is a sensually exciting, impressionistic 10—with Lelouch's less successful sequel, *A Man and a Woman: 20 Years Later*, released in 1986.

The Man Who Fell to Earth
(British Lion) (1976)

In British director Nicholas Roeg's highly original 1976 sci-fi classic, David Bowie delivers an extraordinarily ethereal performance as a lonely alien who splashes down onto Earth in a remote Western lake in the opening sequence. Unlike the mythological Icarus, whose wings melted when he came too close to the sun, this humanoid alien has a mission: to help his compatriots on their distant, dying, drought-stricken planet.

Tall, slender and elegant in demeanor, Thomas Jerome Newton walks into town, sells some gold rings to raise cash and searches out attorney Oliver Farnsworth (Buck Henry) to patent advanced technology electronics products, like a disposable camera that develops its own film. Establishing the World Enterprises Corp. to market these inventions, Newton accumulates enough wealth to build a spaceship to transport water to his home planet, where his family awaits. In the meantime, he meets Mary-Lou (Candy Clark), who distracts him by introducing him to Earthly pleasures like gin-and-tonic and television. But when the CIA becomes suspicious, their idyll is interrupted and he's betrayed, condemned to life on Earth.

Scripted in non-linear fragments by Paul Mayersberg, based on the novel by Walter Tevis, the psychic time-travel story is somewhat confusing and challenging, but cinematographer Anthony Richmond's evocative visual imagery is indelible, particularly the scene in which Newton reveals his extra-terrestrial origin by removing contact lenses and revealing the reptilian eyes beneath.

While casting pop star Bowie in the title role surprised some, Bowie had studied avant-garde theater and mime under Lindsay Kemp before his breakthrough as a musician. He played the role of Cloud in Kemp's 1967 theatrical production *Pierrot in Turquoise* (later made into the 1970 TV film *The Looking Glass Murders*), and in the 1969 black-and-white short *The Image*, Bowie played a ghostly boy who emerges from a disturbed artist's painting to haunt him.

Trawling for trivia, if you look closely, toward the end of the film, in the record store, the disillusioned professor Nathan Bryce (Rip Torn) walks past a display for singer David Bowie's *Young Americans* album, and the music that Oliver Farnsworth is listening to when first glimpsed and last seen is Holst's *The Planets*.

On the Granger Movie Gauge of 1 to 10, *The Man Who Fell to Earth* is an innovative, unique 8. It's thought-provoking and tantalizing.

The Manchurian Candidate
(United Artists) (1962)

This compelling Cold War thriller was considered so politically controversial when it was first released in 1962 that it was either censored or banned in many Eastern European countries under Communist control and even in neutral countries like Finland and Sweden.

When sullen Raymond Shaw (Laurence Harvey) returns from the Korean War as a highly decorated hero, he's described by surviving members of his platoon, including Maj. Bennett Marco (Frank Sinatra), as a warm, wonderful patriot. What they don't realize is that they've all been brainwashed by their Chinese Communist captors in Manchuria.

At the sight of the Queen of Diamonds playing card, Shaw's mind is triggered into obedience, without retaining knowledge of his subsequent actions. His politically ambitious mother (Angela Lansbury) - a diabolical Communist agent posing as a right-wing Republican - plans to have her son shoot the presidential nominee at a Madison Square Garden rally, thus paving the way for her husband, vice-presidential nominee Sen. John Iselin (James Gregory), to take control of the United States government.

Based on a novel by Richard Condon, it was brilliantly adapted by George Axelrod and tautly directed by John Frankenheimer, who said they'd researched every book they could find on the concept of brainwashing, particularly Eugene Kinkead's *Every War but One* (1959).

Frank Sinatra was so eager to play Marco that he flew to Hyannisport in Sept., 1961, to obtain the enthusiastic endorsement of US Pres. John F. Kennedy, which convinced studio president Arthur Krim, an ardent Democrat, to green-light the project. Lucille Ball was Sinatra's original choice for Mrs. Iselin but Frankenheimer convinced him to agree to cast Lansbury who, at 36, was actually only three years older than her 'son,' played by British actor Laurence Harvey. Oscar-nominated Lansbury often credits this contemporary Lady Macbeth role as revitalizing her career.

In real life, the Iselins' private plane was Sinatra's, and the Bar and Grill scene was filmed at a Manhattan restaurant owned by Sinatra's buddy Jilly Rizzo. All the members of Shaw's platoon are named after the cast and crew of "The Phil Silvers Show." And Jonathan Demme's 2004 remake never attained the stature of the original.

On the Granger Movie Gauge of 1 to 10, *The Manchurian Candidate* is a flawlessly executed, high-tension 10, eerily foreshadowing an era of political upheaval and horrifying assassinations.

Mao's Last Dancer
(Samuel Goldwyn Films) (2009)

Think *Billy Elliott* combined with *The Last Emperor* with a touch of *Rocky*. Only a master like Bruce Beresford could envision this sweeping, audacious adaptation of Chinese ballet dancer's Li Cunxin's memoirs with such emotional resonance.

Plucked from his peasant parents (Joan Chen, Wang Shuangbao) in an impoverished rural village in Shandong Province by Communist officials as part of Mao Zedong's Cultural Revolution, eleven-year-old Li is sent to Madame Mao's ballet school in Beijing. Determined to bring pride to his family, perseverant Li embraces the strict, rigorous discipline and is granted the rare privilege of continuing his dance studies in the United States.

Arriving in amazement in Texas as part of an exchange program, he experiences culture-shock but adjusts quickly, deeming his discoveries "fantastic," adopting a different ideology, even falling in love with another dancer (Amanda Schull). Then to the horror of his host/guardian, Ben Stevenson (Bruce Greenwood), artistic director of the Houston Ballet, Li decides to defect, declaring his need to be "free," enrolling an astute attorney (Kyle MacLachlan), and becoming embroiled in a political, emotional and ethical conflict that involves sacrificing all hope of ever seeing his family again.

Australian director Bruce Beresford's films (*Breaker Morant, Tender Mercies, Crimes of the Heart, Driving Miss Daisy*) run an unmatchable gamut but what unites them is an unstoppable cinematic energy that's at the heart of his understated, yet always vigorous style. Jan Sardi's (*Shine*) complex, non-linear screenplay effortlessly shifts between Li's life as a youngster and his present, his childhood experiences and adult dilemmas.

Graeme Murphy's dance sequences soar, and cinematographer Peter James drenches the screen in a torrent of resonating vivid images embodying the sights and sounds of China. As Li Cuxnin at different ages, Chi Cao (principal dancer at Birmingham Royal Ballet), Chengwo Guo (member of Australian Ballet Company) and Huang Wen Bin (aspiring Beijing gymnast) are sensational, as is Bruce Greenwood.

On the Granger Movie Gauge of 1 to 10, *Mao's Last Dancer* is an inspiring, enthralling 10. Great movies transport the audience – and this left me enriched and exhilarated.

March of the Penguins (Warner Independent Pictures) (French) (2005)

French filmmaker Luc Jacquet's nature documentary, narrated by Morgan Freeman, delves into the reproductive lives of the emperor penguins of Antarctica, a barren expanse that explorer Ernest Shackleton described as "the coldest, windiest, driest and darkest continent on the planet."

Each year, emperor penguins who have reached the age of five leave the relative safety of the coastal sea to waddle purposefully 70 miles inland in a single-file procession to their traditional breeding ground where the ice is thick enough to make sure the newborns don't drown. After mating, the female produces a single egg and transfers the nurturing process to the male. While the weary females trudge back to the sea to fill their empty bellies, the males huddle together, waiting for their mates to return.

Often the females die, either from exhaustion or from predators like leopard seals, orcas and giant gull-like petrels. Then the hungry males trek back to the coast. Many chicks die or lose one parent or both during these arduous, repeated journeys back-and-forth in the 71 degrees below zero temperature with winds up to 150-mph.

Once one accepts the appeal of Luc Jacquet's choice to anthropomorphize the penguins' nobility, there's both comedy and drama in their odyssey, amplified by Alex Wurman's upbeat score. These plump, black-and-white birds with a hint of orange on their faces are quite fascinating to watch so, after filming in 16mm for 13 months, the director, cinematographers, editor and writer knew they had a real survival story, a literal race against time.

On the Granger Movie Gauge of 1 to 10, *March of the Penguins* is an eye-popping, endearing 9. If you loved last year's *Winged Migration*, you'll enjoy this G-rated, family-friendly entertainment too.

The Martian (20th Century-Fox) (2015)

Back in 1979, Ridley Scott stunned moviegoers with *Alien*. Now the visual storyteller returns to outer space – with a super-suspenseful saga of an astronaut accidentally stranded on Mars.

When a colossal dust storm forces the Ares 3 crew to abort their Mars surface exploration, Commander Lewis (Jessica Chastain) orders a hasty evacuation, believing their crewmate, Mark Watney (Matt Damon) has been killed by flying debris.

But he's alive, as satellite photography soon reveals. So it's up to NASA director Sanders (Jeff Daniels) and his cohorts at Pasadena's Jet Propulsion Laboratory to figure out how to help Watney stay alive in the habitation module and rescue him before his food supply runs out.

Fortunately, Watney is a resourceful botanist and courageous problem-solver. After removing the shrapnel lodged in his torso, he's faced with basic survival tasks and the necessity of perseverance while facing seemingly insurmountable obstacles.

"I'm gonna have to science the shit out of this," he declares – and proceeds to improvise and innovate, showing a disarmingly acerbic sense of humor. That's evident when he runs out of ketchup and sprinkles crushed Vicodin on his potatoes. But there are always unforeseen catastrophes.

Screenwriter Drew Goddard (*World War Z*) has adapted Andy Weir's 2011 novel, as director Ridley Scott meticulously delineates Watney's ingenuity in his struggle to endure. He's a plausible Robinson Crusoe, tossing around geek speak terms like hexadecimals and orbital trajectories.

Filmgoers may recall Matt Damon did an uncredited 'bit' as a stranded astronaut in *Interstellar*, but here his charming, utterly convincing performance propels the drama on a desolate planet.

Chiwetel Ejiofor, Sean Bean, Kristen Wiig, Donald Glover and Macenzie Davis score as supportive scientists – with a nod to *Lord of the Rings* – while Kate Mara, Michael Pena, Sebastian Stan and Aksel Hennie comprise the Ares 3 team.

Reminiscent of solo tales like *Gravity, Cast Away*, and *Moon*, it should certainly engender enthusiasm for the future of space travel, as NASA strives to send humans to Mars by the 2030s.

> On the Granger Movie Gauge of 1 to 10, *The Martian* is an exhilarating 8—an enthralling sci-fi adventure.

Marvel's The Avengers (Walt Disney / Paramount Pictures) (2012)

Marvel Studios has been preparing audiences for this thrilling, collaborative action-adventure for the past few years, beginning with *Iron Man* and continuing with its sequel-- plus *The Incredible Hulk*, *Thor*, and *Captain America: The First Avenger*.

Global annihilation is imminent when Thor's brazen, bitter brother, Loki (Tom Hiddleston), arrives on Earth from Asgard and swipes the energy-packed Tesseract, an all-powerful Cosmic Cube, discovered on the ocean's bottom in *Captain America*, through which he can summon intergalactic alien invaders. That's why eye-patched Nick Fury (Samuel L. Jackson) overrules his colleagues in the international peace-keeping agency known as S.H.I.E.L.D, and summons the disparate yet similarly egocentric, spandex-clad superheroes to a summit aboard his enormous airship.

Snarky playboy billionaire Tony Stark/Iron Man (Robert Downey Jr.) immediately spars with the earnest, no-nonsense W.W. II hero Steve Rogers/Captain America (Chris Evans), along with the straight-laced, imperious, hammer-wielding Nordic god Thor (Chris Hemsworth). Fury's sultry, covert operative Natasha Romanoff/Black Widow (Scarlett Johansson) has a vested interest in breaking Loki's spell on her archer/assassin ally, Clint Barton/Hawkeye (Jeremy Renner), while world-weary scientist Bruce Banner/Hulk (Mark Ruffalo), tracking the Cube's radiation, struggles to control the curse of his terrible temper.

Based on series created by Stan Lee (who does a cameo in the climactic chaos) and Jack Kelly, it was scripted by Zak Penn and re-written by director Joss Whedon (*The Cabin in the Woods*, TV's *Buffy: The Vampire Slayer*), combining sly, snappy dialogue with an awesome special-effects, particularly in the massive battle in midtown Manhattan. Seamus McGarvey's cinematography is superb, along with Alan Silvestri's score. Plus, there's Gwyneth Paltrow as Pepper Potts, Stellan Skarsgard as Professor Erik Selvig, Paul Bettany as Jarvis with Clark Gregg and Cobie Smulders as Agents Phil Colson and Maria Hill. In post-production, it was digitally converted to 3D and re-mastered for IMAX 3D.

On the Granger Movie Gauge of 1 to 10, *Marvel's The Avengers* is an amusing, entertaining 9 - for those who have been eagerly anticipating the familiarly iconic, comic-book-based superstar line-up. And remember to stay through the credits.

M*A*S*H* (20ᵗʰ Century-Fox) (1972)

Set in 1951, during the Korean War, but made at the height of the Vietnam War, Robert Altman's anti-war comedy/drama follows the fortunes of the 4077th MASH (Mobile Army Surgical Hospital). It begins with the arrival of fun-loving, rebellious, irreverent Capt. "Hawkeye" Pierce (Donald Sutherland) and Capt. "Duke" Forrest (Tom Skerritt). They immediately clash with chief surgical nurse Maj. Margaret "Hot Lips" Houlihan (Sally Kellerman) and their priggish tent-mate, Maj. Frank Burns (Robert Duvall).

When Hawkeye and Duke request a thoracic specialist, Capt. "Trapper" John McIntyre (Elliott Gould) joins the unit. Compassionate and capable surgeons, the trio pull a variety of pranks, including broadcasting a Burns/Houlihan lovemaking session over the public address system and collapsing the women's shower, revealing naked Maj. Houlihan.

Based on Richard Hooker's semi-autobiographical *MASH: A Novel About Three Army Doctors*, it was episodically scripted by Ring Lardner Jr. and directed by Robert Altman, whose unorthodox innovations included overlapping dialogue, clever camera set-ups, and inventive sight gags. This bleak, black comedy delivers a poignant portrait of the insanity of war and – in his director's commentary on the DVD release – Altman says this was the first major studio film to use the word "fuck' in its dialogue. As Walter "Radar" O'Reilly, Gary Burghoff played the same character in the movie and the popular TV series that ran from 1972 to 1983. As General Hammond, G. Wood also appeared in the first three episodes of the TV series. The franchise concluded with the spinoff *Trapper John, M.D.* in 1986.

Nominated in 1970 for five Academy Awards, it won an Oscar for its screenplay. In Stephen M. Silverman's *The Fox That Got Away*, Robert Altman confessed that he got $75,000 for doing *M*A*S*H*, while the studio made $1 billion from it. The reason he didn't get a percentage of the gross was because Grace Kelly went to Fox's Board of Directors and said, "Don't dare give that man a penny for that terrible movie!" No one confirmed or denied that statement, yet it's known that Dennis Stanfill, a friend of Princess Grace's, joined the Fox Board in the early 1970s.

As a result, Robert Altman's son, Mike Altman, who wrote the lyrics to the "Suicide is Painless" theme song at age 14, reportedly made more money from the franchise than his father ever did.

On the Granger Movie Gauge of 1 to 10, *M*A*S*H** is a satirical 10, effectively launching Robert Altman's career.

Match Point (DreamWorks) (2005)

Woody Allen gets his groove back by leaving New York and creating his best film in years.

Set in London, this psychological thriller revolves around ambitious Chris Wilton (Jonathan Rhys-Meyers), a rather unscrupulous, Irish working-class tennis pro who marries Chloe Hewett (Emily Mortimer), the sweetly pampered daughter of a posh, privileged English banking family, while casually falling in love with his amiable brother-in-law's sexy blonde fiancé Nola Rice (Scarlett Johansson), a struggling, self-doubting American actress. But much to the besotted cad's horror, their torrid affair leads to a ruthless and terrifying ultimatum from the neurotic, increasingly desperate femme fatale: either leave your wife – or else!

The film's poignant undercurrent is the capricious concept of dumb luck, noting, "The man who said, 'I'd rather be lucky than good,' saw deeply into life. People are afraid to face how great a part of life is dependent on luck. It's scary to think so much is out of one's control."

While maintaining a subversive comedic banter amid the *Crimes and Misdemeanors* meets Alfred Hitchcock-like concept, Woody Allen captures the wistful, melancholy tone, utilizing London's gray, often cloudy skies, working with an almost exclusively British cast and crew, including cinematographer Remi Adefarasin and production designer Jim Clay. And the vintage operatic soundtrack of Donizetti and Verdi supplies an intriguing counterpoint to the melodrama. The adroitly cast actors are excellent, particularly Scarlett Johansson (*The Island*) who has already signed on for Allen's next film, *Scoop*, a romantic comedy.

On the Granger Movie Gauge of 1 to 10, *Match Point* is a chilling, riveting, mind-teasing 10, one of the best of 2005.

Meet Me in St. Louis (M.G.M.) (1944)

There's no better chronicle of homespun, middle-class America at the turn-of-the-previous-century than this simple, nostalgic story of a closely-knit St. Louis, Missouri, family on the eve of the 1904 World's Fair, the Louisiana Purchase Exposition. Dwelling at 5135 Kensington Avenue are Alonzo Smith (Leon Ames), his wife (Mary Astor), their son Lon Jr. (Henry H. Daniels Jr.) and four daughters - Rose (Lucille Bremer), Esther (Judy Garland), Agnes (Joan Carroll) and incorrigible, troublemaking Tootie (Margaret O'Brien). Harry Davenport plays Grandpa with Marjorie Main as the Smiths' outspoken maid.

While Rose is expecting a proposal from her Yale beau, Warren Sheffield (Robert Sully), Esther is smitten by John Truett (Tom Drake), the handsome boy-next-door. Complications arise, particularly when there's a good chance that the family will have to re-locate to New York. And the sentimental finale takes place overlooking the Grand Lagoon just as thousands of lights illuminate the opening of the World's Fair.

Based on Sally Benson's short stories published in *The New Yorker*, it was adapted into a screenplay by Irving Brecher and Fred Finklehoffe with splendid songs by Hugh Martin and Ralph Blane, arranged by Conrad Salinger. As soon as director Vincente Minnelli met Judy Garland, he fell in love and they subsequently married, making four more films together before divorcing in 1951. Their daughter Liza Minnelli has said: "You can see his love for her in every frame. It's my favorite for – when all is said and done – I wouldn't be here if it weren't for that movie."

Introduced with the movie in 1944, Judy Garland's musical numbers such as "The Boy Next Door" and "The Trolley Song" gained immediate popularity, and "Have Yourself a Merry Little Christmas" became a perennial holiday classic. The songs "Skip to My Lou" and "Under the Bamboo Tree" were period favorites, and MGM producer Arthur Freed dubbed Leon Ames' signing voice for the "You and I" number because Minnelli wanted the father to sound 'real,' not trained.

This was Vincente Minnelli's first Technicolor film, setting his cinematic style. He envisioned it looking like Thomas Eakins's paintings, dividing the structure of the film into four impressionistic seasons.

On the Granger Movie Gauge of 1 to 10, *Meet Me in St. Louis* is an entrancing 10, reflecting a bygone era.

Midnight in Paris
(Sony Pictures Classics) (2011)

In this fanciful fable, writer/director Woody Allen ruminates on nostalgia: a bittersweet longing for idealized things, persons or situations of the past.

Successful-but-dissatisfied Hollywood screenwriter Gil Pender (Owen Wilson) is in Paris, diligently working on his first novel, yet insecure about his serious literary ability. His protagonist runs a memorabilia shop and, like Gil, wistfully yearns to have lived back in the 1920s, the unabashedly romantic era reflected in Cole Porter's music. One night, as Gil is walking back to the hotel by himself after dinner in a restaurant with his shrill fiancée (Rachel McAdams) and her bourgeois parents (Mimi Kennedy, Kurt Fuller), an extraordinary thing happens.

As the clock strikes midnight, a vintage yellow Peugeot pulls up and a festive young couple beckons him inside. To his amazement, it's Zelda and F. Scott Fitzgerald, drinking Dom Perignon and inviting him to join them at a party. Thanks to magical realism, it turns out to be the most amazing evening of Gil's life, as he hobnobs with the cultural and artistic giants of the Lost Generation, along with a lovely damsel (Marion Cotillard) who, in turn, yearns for the Belle Epoque. Eager to repeat the incredible experience, Gil returns to the same street at midnight, night after night. To tell you whom he meets, what they say to him and what happens would ruin the surprise.

Charming, shaggy Owen Wilson epitomizes Woody Allen's idealistic and self-absorbed sensibilities. The illusion-versus-reality concept evokes memories of *Purple Rose of Cairo* in which a mousy housewife (Mia Farrow) flees from the brutality of real life into the imaginary world of movies, along with the Americans-abroad ambiance of *Vicky Cristina Barcelona*. The acting ensemble is superb, particularly Kathy Bates as Gertrude Stein, Corey Stoll as Ernest Hemingway and Adrien Brody as Salvador Dali. In a cameo, French First Lady Carla Bruni-Sarkozy is a Rodin Museum tour guide.

On the Granger Movie Gauge of 1 to 10, *Midnight in Paris* is an amusing, whimsical, time-traveling 10, an inventive cinematic celebration of the iconic City of Lights.

Mission Impossible: Rogue Nation (Paramount Pictures/Skydance) (2015)

FULL DISCLOSURE: My son, Don Granger, produced this movie.

This fifth incarnation of the *Mission Impossible* franchise begins with a spectacular, pulse-pounding stunt in which IMF agent Ethan Hunt climbs aboard a huge A-400 cargo plane as it's taking off.

Yes, that's really Tom Cruise! And the thrill-ride fun is just beginning...

Ethan is in the middle of a mission when he discovers that a stealthy group of terrorists, known as The Syndicate, led by coldly sinister Solomon Lane (Sean Harris), are working discredit the IMF by insidiously recruiting former intelligence operatives from around the world to destabilize countries and 'eliminate' major international figures.

The problem is no one believes him, particularly incoming CIA chief, Alan Huntley (Alec Baldwin), who discredits him and the entire operation.

Enter mysterious Ilsa Faust (Rebecca Ferguson), a lithe femme fatale, ostensibly from Britain's MI6, who has infiltrated the Syndicate, yet may or may not be playing both sides. But since she resourcefully saves Ethan's life – not once but twice – that earns her some credibility with suspicious IMF operatives (Jeremy Renner, Ving Rhames, Simon Pegg).

Adding unexpected touches of humor, writer/director Christopher McQuarrie (*Jack Reacher*) superbly crafts the intricate, fast-paced espionage suspense, building to several dynamic highpoints, elegantly photographed by Robert Elswit.

There's an eye-popping assassination attempt in the Vienna Opera House during a performance of Puccini's *Turandot*; Ethan's daring dive into a whirling maelstrom, holding his breath during a perilous underwater retrieval; and an intrepid car-and-bike chase in Morocco – plus other stunning surprises along the way.

Effectively at the top of his game, vital-yet-vulnerable Tom Cruise is heroically resilient, often matched stunt-for-stunt by stunning Sweden's Rebecca Ferguson, whose name 'Ilse' evokes memories of another enigmatic Swede, Ingrid Bergman, in *Casablanca*. Fittingly, Joe Kraemer's propulsive score includes strains of Lalo Schifrin's original TV series theme.

On the Granger Movie Gauge of 1 to 10, *Mission Impossible: Rogue Nation* is a taut 10, the most exciting action-adventure of the summer.

Moneyball (Columbia Pictures/Sony) (2011)

Superficially, you could call this a baseball movie. But it's about far more than that, opening with a quote from Yankees great Mickey Mantle: "It's unbelievable how much you don't know about a game you've been playing your whole life."

As a hotshot high school athlete, young Billy Beane faced a difficult choice: a full scholarship to Stanford University or a chance to play for the New York Mets. In rueful recollection, he regards his decision to sign with the Mets as the only decision he would ever make in his life about money.

After his playing career prematurely fizzled, Billy (Brad Pitt) worked his way from scout to general manager of the underdog Oakland Athletics, only to relinquish his three top players (Jason Giambi, Johnny Damon, Jason Isringhausen) to the big-money franchises of New York and Boston in 2001, after losing the American League division series. Unable to compete for high-priced athletes, Billy hooks up with Peter Brand (Jonah Hill), a nerdy numbers-cruncher with an economics degree from Yale.

Convinced that baseball's conventional wisdom is wrong, Brand devises a sabermetric, or quantitative, approach to scouting players, based on Bill James's pioneering statistical analysis. Convinced this unconventional concept may work, Billy signs undervalued players from across the country, assembling what Brand calls "an island of misfit toys." Defying his development people, including surly, stubborn team manager Art Howe (Philip Seymour Hoffman) and risking his career, Billy reinvents professional baseball.

Adapted by Steve Zaillian (*Schindler's List*) and Aaron Sorkin (*The Social Network*) from Michael Lewis's best-seller and directed with focused, assured vision by Bennett Miller (*Capote*), it's an inspiring, underdog story, set in Big League ballparks. Oozing charisma, Brad Pitt delivers an astonishingly accomplished performance, embodying brooding Billy Beane, a divorced dad who's devoted to his teenage daughter (Kerris Dorsey), while Jonah Hill's geeky Brant displays a slow, subtle accumulation of precisely observed details, culminating in a brilliantly understated effort.

On the Granger Movie Gauge of 1 to 10, *Moneyball* slugs a terrific 10 out of the batter's box and generating considerable Oscar buzz.

Monsoon Wedding (USA Films) (2001)

Harvard-educated Indian filmmaker Mira Nair (*Mississippi Masala, Salaam Bombay!)* transports us far away to New Delhi to the exhilarating nuptials of a beautiful young Punjabi woman in this intimate exploration of the contemporary culture clashes in this exotic rite-of-passage.

Aditi Verma (Vasundhara Das) is the only daughter of a hyper tense, upper middle-class businessman (Naseeruddin Shah) who has arranged for her to marry a Texas-based engineer (Psarin Dabas) and move to America. Problem is: she's never met her fiancé and is still having an affair with a married TV talk-show host. Despite the sweltering heat, relatives arrive from all over the world as the lavish marriage preparations proceed at a feverish pitch.

Like a Robert Altman film, there's a sprawling cast of disparate characters whose lives are interlinked. Like the mercurial event planner (Vijay Raaz) who falls in love with the Vermas's shy, virtuous maid (Tilotama Shome); a cousin (Neha Dubey) who's after another cousin (Randeep Hooda) back from school in Sydney; and another unmarried cousin (Shefali Shetty) who yearns be a writer but who, ultimately, bears her emotional scars to reveal a shameful, sorrowful secret.

Using English, Hindi and Punjabi, screenwriter Sabrina Dhawan cleverly interweaves old customs and westernization within the raunchy, robust, resplendent festivities. Photographed by Declan Quinn, it's a sensual delight—with pop-jazz-folk music, sumptuous food and a plethora of orange marigolds, the Indian wedding flower. It's easy to understand why it won the Golden Lion, the top prize at the Venice Film Festival.

On the Granger Movie Gauge of 1 to 10, *Monsoon Wedding* is an insightful, intoxicating 9, offering a fresh look at the universality and complexity of human relationships.

The Motorcycle Diaries (Focus Features) (2004)

Brazilian director Walter Salles' inspiring adaptation of Ernesto "Che" Guevara's memoirs chronicles the young Argentine doctor's 1952 coming-of-age trip up the western coast of South America, through Chile, Peru and the Amazon to Venezuela, on a dilapidated Norton 500 motorbike with his buddy, Alberto Granado. It's an eight-month, 8,000-mile journey of self-discovery that will change both of their lives forever.

As the trip begins, sensitive, soulful Ernesto (Gael Garcia Bernal), an asthmatic twenty-three-year-old, and Alberto (Rodrigo De La Serna), a chubby, carousing twenty-nine-year-old biochemist, seek adventure – and they find it. When Ernesto's virginal girlfriend rebuffs him, he irresponsibly flirts with a married woman, necessitating a hasty departure from a small Chilean town.

As they travel, along with the abundant, light-hearted frivolity, however, comes Ernesto's growing frustration with social inequity, particularly towards the impoverished indigenous people, descendants of the once-great Inca civilization that dominated the Andes. "So much injustice," he notes. With an elegant, stunning visuality, Salles and screenwriter Jose Rivera not only capture the drama and earnest idealism of a time and a place but also what inspired Ernesto's revolutionary fervor, transforming his destiny. Leisurely episodic in nature, it relishes both the harshness and the romance of buddies on the open road while subtly planting Ernesto's political roots.

In Spanish with subtitles, the performances are strong enough to overcome the language barrier.

On the Granger Movie Gauge of 1 to 10, *The Motorcycle Diaries* is a tender, haunting 9, concluding with the indelible image of the now eighty-two-year-old Dr. Alberto Granado.

Mr. Deeds Goes to Town
(Columbia Studios) (1936)

Producer/director Frank Capra's success coincided with America's Great Depression, when he became Hollywood's champion of the "common man."

Inspired by a magazine serial *Opera Hat* by Clarence Budington Kelland, Robert Riskin and Frank Capra (collaborators on *It Happened One Night*) were intrigued by the idea of Longfellow Deeds (Gary Cooper), a greeting-card poet from Mandrake Falls, Vermont, inheriting a vast fortune – which, in 1936, was 20 million dollars.

"I wonder why he left me all that money. I don't need it," Deeds says. His benefactor's scheming attorney, John Cedar (Douglas Dumbrille), brings him to New York City, where cynical press agent Cornelius Cobb (Lionel Stander) tries to shield him from the press. But tabloid reporter Louise "Babe" Bennett (Jean Arthur) gets through to him, masquerading as a poor worker. Deceitfully gaining Deeds' confidence, she publishes a series of derisive articles, dubbing him "Cinderella Man."

Nevertheless, Deeds is determined to use his windfall to help the poor, even though the lawyers are trying to have him declared insane. That leads to a hilarious yet inspiring show-down, including Deeds' testimony: "Seems like a lot of fuss has been made about my playing the tuba. If a man's crazy just because he plays the tuba, then somebody'd better look into it because there are a lot of tuba players running around."

Previously, Gary Cooper had been cast as a sex symbol, sharing sizzling love scenes with Joan Crawford and Marlene Dietrich. But here he establishes himself as quintessential honest, homespun all-American male. According to Capra, "Every line in his face spelled honesty. So innate was his integrity, he could be cast in phony parts but never look phony himself. Tall, gaunt as Lincoln, cast in the frontier mold of Daniel Boone, Sam Houston, Kit Carson, this silent Montana cow-puncher embodied all the true-blue virtues that won the West: durability, honesty and native intelligence."

Nominated for five Academy Awards, it won only one: Frank Capra received the Oscar as Best Director. It was noted that Capra was President of the Academy at the time and had been fighting against the unionization of actors and directors.

On the Granger Movie Gauge of 1 to 10, *Mr. Deeds Goes to Town* is an absurdly endearing 10. It's a screwball comedy that makes a social statement—along with introducing the words "pixilated" and "doodle" to the vocabulary.

Mr. Smith Goes to Washington (Columbia Pictures) (1939)

Savoring the success of *It Happened One Night, You Can't Take It with You* and *Mr. Deeds Goes to Town*, producer/director Frank Capra tackled the story of an Everyman who becomes embroiled in the darkest aspects of Washington's politics.

In his autobiography, *The Name Above the Title*, Capra revealed: "The first thing we did in our Capital City was to go rubbernecking in a sightseeing bus. We wanted to see Washington just as our dewy-eyed freshman Senator would see it..."

Jimmy Stewart plays gullible Jefferson Smith, an idealistic junior Senator who naively takes on the decadent political system when powerful businessman Jim Taylor (Edward Arnold) and his nameless state's senior Senator Joseph Paine (Claude Raines) oppose a bill that would build a much needed national boys' camp on land that they'd ear-marked for a dam-building graft scheme. (When the Boy Scouts of America refused to allow their name to be used, Smith advocated for the Boy Rangers.) Refusing to be bribed or intimated by defamatory accusations—and supported by his secretary, Clarissa Saunders (Jean Arthur) —Smith filibusters, talking non-stop for 23 hours until he's utterly exhausted.

In order to simulate Mr. Smith's hoarseness, Stewart consulted a throat doctor who dropped dichloride of mercury into his throat, not near his vocal chords, on the set. His supporting cast included some of Hollywood's best character actors: Thomas Mitchell, William Demarest, H.B. Warner and Harry Carey, who was nominated as Best Supporting Actor.

Dismayed Joseph P. Kennedy, the American Ambassador to Great Britain - and father of future President John F. Kennedy - cabled Capra and Columbia Studio head Harry Cohn that he feared the film would damage "America's prestige in Europe." While it was bitterly denounced by him and Washington insiders for its allegations of corruption, the film was banned by Europe's Fascist states that were afraid it confirmed that democracy works.

In 1939, considered the finest year in Hollywood history, *Mr. Smith Goes to Washington* garnered 10 nominations but won only for Sidney Buchman's screenplay, based on Lewis R. Foster's unpublished story. Other contenders were *Gone with the Wind, Dark Victory, Goodbye Mr. Chips, Love Affair, Ninotchka, Of Mice and Men, Stagecoach,* and *The Wizard of Oz.*

On the Granger Movie Gauge of 1 to 10, *Mr. Smith Goes to Washington* is a timely, whistle-blowing 9, showing the difference that one determined individual can make.

Notting Hill (Polygram/Universal Pictures release) (1999)

She's the most dazzling, famous movie star in the world and he's the sheepish, fumbling proprietor of a tiny travel book store on funky Notting Hill in London. Can they fall in love? Why not? In this joyous, contemporary fairy tale, anything's possible. Especially with a script by Richard Curtis (*Four Weddings and a Funeral*) that's reminiscent of Audrey Hepburn's *Roman Holiday*.

The set-up has Julia Roberts, a glamorous American actress, meet Hugh Grant, a bookseller, in his shop—after which he inadvertently spills orange juice all over her T-shirt. She agrees to let him awkwardly clean her up in his nearby flat and—well, nature takes its course. But their path to romance has plenty of bumps which I won't ruin for you. Suffice it to say, she's the impetuous aggressor, while he's wary. She's sophisticated; he's shy.

She's agile; he's clumsy. She's direct, saying whatever she thinks; he's understated and evasive, musing, "I've opened Pandora's box, and there's trouble inside."

Director Roger Michell has astutely assembled a superb British supporting cast, particularly Rhys Ifans as Grant's wild, Welsh flat-mate and Emma Chambers as his ditsy sister, with Alec Baldwin in an uncredited cameo as Roberts' boy-friend who drops in unexpectedly. There are several mischievous sequences involving the absolute idiocy people display in the presence of a celebrity and a comic sparring-match with the British tabloid press, plus a timely scandal involving obscene photos and sly, amusing repartee involving Mel Gibson's bottom.

> On the Granger Movie Gauge of 1 to 10, *Notting Hill* is an amusing, captivating, relentlessly entertaining 10 – a perfect date movie and one of the most delightful films in years!

Pan's Labyrinth (Picturehouse) (2006)

In *Pan's Labyrinth*, writer/director Guillermo del Toro has created one of the most fascinating, imaginative yet darkly disturbing political fables of our time.

In 1944 during Spanish Civil War, a ten-year-old girl, Ofelia (Ivana Baquero), travels with her delicate, pregnant mother Carmen (Ariadna Gil) to meet her arrogant, terrifying new stepfather, Captain Vidal (Sergi Lopez), in an old mill in the mountains of northern Spain, where Franco's fascist troops, under his sadistic command, are killing what's left of the Republican resistance. Ofelia's only comfort comes from the captain's housekeeper, Mercedes (Maribel Verdu), who is secretly helping the partisan guerrillas.

Lonely and faced with unspeakable brutality, Ofelia retreats into a fairy story in which the legendary pagan faun Pan (mime Doug Jones) greets her in a hidden underground world beneath a crumbling stone labyrinth in the garden. He tells her she's a lost princess and assigns her three tasks – challenges that include facing a giant toad to deceiving a pale, faceless ogre with eyes in his hands while ignoring a banquet at which she must not eat or drink anything. Then there's the mysterious mandrake root she must place in a bowl of milk beneath her sickly mother's bed and feed with drops of blood. But Ofelia is torn by a need to rebel against authority.

Evoking *Alice in Wonderland* and *The Chronicles of Narnia*, yet stunningly original, this sinister, surreal, strangely grotesque, R-rated fable is filled with magical, sometimes scary special effects and visuals, not unlike tales from the Brothers Grimm. And the acting is captivating.

On the Granger Movie Gauge of 1 to 10, *Pan's Labyrinth* is an enchanting, wondrous, fantastical 10. Don't be put off because it's in Spanish with English subtitles. Like *Il Postino* (*The Postman*), it transcends language.

The Pianist (Focus Features) (2002)

Based on celebrated composer/pianist Wladyslaw Szpilman's 1946 memoir, *Death of a City*, this epic Holocaust-survivor story revolves around the plight of a talented musician who was playing piano on Polish state radio when Hitler's Luftwaffe attacked Warsaw in September, 1939.

At first unbelieving, Wladyslaw (Adrien Brody) and his family struggle to maintain some semblance of a lifestyle within the cruel, humiliating restrictions imposed on the half-million Jews who were herded into the walled Ghetto. However, it soon becomes apparent that they're doomed to slaughter on the streets or in the death camp. Only Wladyslaw manages to escape the brutal, mandatory deportation.

Aided by admirers, he's sheltered from capture by a series of sympathizers and Resistance fighters who hide him in attics or cellars until he's forced to fend for himself —once, by pretending to be a corpse. In one subtle yet astonishing sequence, he's discovered by a Nazi officer who, miraculously, decides not to turn him in, choosing, instead, to listen—transfixed—as he plays a concerto. Director Roman Polanski (who as a child escaped from the Ghetto by crawling through a hole in a barbed-wire fence), screenwriter Ronald Harwood, cinematographer Pawel Edelman and production designer Allan Starski (Oscar-winner for *Schindler's List*) impeccably re-create the atrocities of that sad, horrifying era of 20th-century history.

As for the ultimate fate of the subject, Wladyslaw Szpilman, he died at 88 in 2000.

Although not on a level with *Schindler's List*, on the Granger Movie Gauge of 1 to 10, *The Pianist* is a haunting 9. For those who enjoy trivia: the little girl carrying the empty bird cage in a crowd scene is Polanski's eleven-year-old daughter Morgan; it's a poignant moment comparable to Steven Spielberg's "the girl with the red dress."

Quartet (The Weinstein Company) (2012)

Not to be confused with the similarly titled *A Late Quartet*, this deliciously tart comedy is, essentially, a British film that revives the old Mickey Rooney/Judy Garland "let's put on a show" formula with great panache.

Set in the bucolic English countryside, Beecham House, an elegant retirement refuge for musicians, is facing dire financial straits just as a new resident unexpectedly moves in. It's famed soloist Jean Horton (Maggie Smith). But she's in no mood to socialize. While her arrival stuns longtime resident Reginald Paget (Tom Courtenay), her cuckolded-and-heart-broken former husband who now devotes his time to making opera relevant for youthful rappers, it delights ebullient, somewhat senile Cecily Robson (Pauline Collins), her former singing partner.

The burning question revolves around whether the haughty, sharp-tongued diva will agree to participate in the upcoming Giuseppe Verdi's birthday fund-raising concert with her old cohorts. Observing from the sidelines are perennially lecherous rake Wilfred Bond (Scottish comedian Billy Connolly), egotistically cranky Cedric Livingston (Michael Gambon), rival soprano Anne Langley (opera great Gwyneth Jones) and amiably solicitous Dr. Lucy Cogan (Sheridan Smith).

Scripted by Ronald Harwood (*The Pianist*), who adapted his 1999 *Ageing is not for Sissies* stage play, it's adroitly directed by Dustin Hoffman, who encouraged his distinguished cast to improvise dialogue, thereby eliciting sensitive, indelibly individualistic performances. The ensemble also includes many real-life musicians, including former Grammy-winners and a past conductor of the London symphony, who enthusiastically perform classical selections from *Rigoletto* and *La Traviata*, punctuated by Dario Marianelli's effective score. It's worth staying for their salute during the concluding credits.

A recent Kennedy Center Award honoree for acting, Dustin Hoffman makes an auspicious directorial debut with this classy, uplifting crowd-pleaser, which is reminiscent of Daniel Schmid's 1985 documentary about retired Italian opera singers living together in the Casa Riposo per Musicisti—a.k.a. *Casa Verdi*.

On the Granger Movie Gauge of 1 to 10, *Quartet* is an endearing, astutely engaging 8, joining *The Best Exotic Marigold Hotel* in chronicling life's third act.

Raise the Red Lantern (M.G.M.) (Mandarin) (1991)

As leader of China's rebellious Fifth Generation directors who began working after the Cultural Revolution, Zhang Yimou often sets his films in the feudal past, subtly tweaking the still-enduring politics of power and authoritarian control.

In northern China in the 1920s, the intrigue begins as a nineteen-year-old student, Songlian (Gong Li), arrives at a sprawling feudal compound belonging to the Chen family. Forced into marriage by her stepmother, Songlian is the Fourth Mistress of a regal warlord (Ma Jingwu), who is so wealthy enough to provide a separate home for each of his wives. Ruled by elaborate rituals, the resentful women often dine together, anxiously waiting to find out who will be chosen as their mutual husband/master's companion for night. The preferred female is not only given a sensuous foot massage but she also has the customary privilege of choosing the mealtime menu, while the servants ceremonially hang red lanterns outside her abode as visible sign of her dominance and favor.

"If you can manage to have a foot massage every day, you'll soon be running this household," Songlian is informed by the Second Mistress, Zhuoyun (Cao Cuifeng). As she establishers her position, she becomes aware of the treachery within their cloistered existence. Songlian is particularly resented by the Third Mistress, Meishan (He Caifei), a scheming, spoiled former opera singer, and the ranking Chen maid Yan'er (Kong Lin), who has ambitions to become a Mistress someday herself, but not Yuru (Jin Shuyuan), who is older and, as Chan's First Mistress, has rank.

Trained in cinematography at the Beijing Film Academy, Zhang Yimou (*Red Sorgum, Ju Dou*) made the transition to director with great assurance, particularly with beautiful Gong Li as his leading lady. This opulent, visually stunning, startlingly feminist melodrama, written by Ni Zhen, based on the novel *Wives and Concubines* by Su Tong, was filmed in Qiao's Compound near the ancient city of Pingyao in Shanxi Province.

On the Granger Movie Gauge of 1 to 10, *Raise the Red Lantern* is an enthralling, revelatory 10. A 1992 Oscar-nominee for Best Foreign Language Film, the story was later adapted by Zhang Yimou into an acclaimed dance of the same title for the National Ballet of China.

Rashomon (RKO Radio Pictures) (1950)

It allegedly took two years for writer/director Akira Kurosawa to convince Daiei Motion Pictures to finance this cryptic crime drama and, even after the picture was completed, production executives were stunned when it was awarded the Golden Lion at the Venice Film Festival in 1951. That accolade brought this impressionistic endeavor to the attention of American audiences, who had been reluctant to accept Japanese films since W.W.II. Subsequently, it won an honorary Academy Award as Best Foreign Film.

Set in 19th century Kyoto, four people involved in a rape/murder tell varying, mutually contradictory versions of what happened, as Kurosawa examines the nature of human nature and truth, asserting that what we believe to be depends on how we see it, who is seeing it, and who is telling it.

Adapted from short stories by Ryunosuke Akutagawa and astutely filmed by Kazuo Miyagawa, the assault is repeatedly reenacted, as a nobleman's bride is raped by a bandit, and the husband is either murdered or commits suicide. Machiko Kyo is the victim; Toshiro Mifune is the bandit; Masaykui Mori is the deceased samurai, speaking through a medium; and Takashi Shimura is the woodcutter witness.

According to reports, when Kurosawa was filming, his actors and crew lived together, allowing bonding and collaborative exchange that would otherwise not have been possible. He insisted on shooting with several cameras at once so that he could have a variety of choices when he was editing. Composer Fumio Hayasaka created the music, including a haunting variation on Maurice Ravel's *Bolero* as the woman relates her story.

Kurosawa's minimalist, non-linear approach, and his technique of shooting directly into the sun and utilizing mirrors to reflect sunlight onto the actors' faces, influenced American directors like Francis Ford Coppola, Paul Schroder, George Lucas, and others. This complex story became *The Outrage*, a Broadway play starring Rod Steiger and a 1964 film starring Paul Newman.

On the Granger Movie Gauge of 1 to 10, *Rashomon* is a purposefully enigmatic 10, creating the term *Rashomon* as an integral part of our film-referential language.

Ratatouille (Buena Vista/Disney) (2007)

Ratatouille is delicious! Who would believe this rat-turned-chef gastronomical caper could capture the culinary heart of the City of Lights?

Cultured, educated and blessed with acute sensibilities, Remy (voiced by comedian Patton Oswalt) is a thin blue rat who lives with his rodent relatives in the French country-side. But he's different. Remy's taste buds are more cultivated; he prefers haute cuisine to garbage. So when disaster strikes and the family is forced to flee through the sewers, it's not surprising that Remy winds up in Paris near a restaurant that belonged to a legendary chef, Auguste Gusteau (Brad Garrett), who proclaimed, "Anyone can cook!"

Intrigued and sensually intoxicated, Remy sneaks in and spices up a vat of soup ostensibly cooked by Linguini (Lou Romano), a garbage boy who's ordered by the sous chef (Ian Holm) to reproduce it as a menu staple.

Realizing his ineptitude, Linguini reluctantly teams up with Remy, forming an unlikely partnership (filled with slapstick shtick) that must be kept secret from everyone, including adorably coquettish Colette (Janeane Garofalo), the lone female cook, and a caustic restaurant critic, Anton Ego (Peter O'Toole—at his haughty nastiest).

Conceived and co-directed by Jan Pinkava (*A Bug's Life*) with screenwriter/director Brad Bird (*The Incredibles*), it's filled with perfectly paced yet subtle character humor and heart, emerging as another Oscar-tempting Disney/Pixar creation. The meticulously detailed animation is stunning, subtly shifting between the rodent and human perspectives – and the mouth-watering food is temptingly textured.

Historically, Disney has built much of its reputation on romping rodents—beginning with Mickey and Minnie Mouse and rollicking through *The Rescuers*, as well as *Cinderella*. On the Granger Movie Gauge of 1 to 10, *Ratatouille* (pronounced by Pixar as "rat-a-too-ee") is a captivating, inventive, soufflé-light 10. Family audiences will eat it up!

The Red Shoes (J. Arthur Rank/Universal Pictures) (1948)

Without doubt the most emotionally engaging and technically brilliant ballet film ever made, this 1948 production is loosely based on Hans Christian Andersen's fable and inspired by the real-life meeting between Sergei Diaghilev and Diana Gould. Reportedly, the Russian impresario invited the British ballerina to join his Ballets Russes but he died before she could comply; Gould later became the second wife of musician Yehudi Menuhin.

Written, directed and produced by Michael Powell and Emeric Pressburger, a partnership known as The Archers, it's a bittersweet, romantic story-within-a-story. Aristocratic Victoria 'Vicky' Page (Moira Shearer) is a young, unknown dancer who meets charismatic Boris Lermontov (Anton Walbrook) of the Ballet Lermontov. Appreciating her talent, Lermontov creates a starring role for her in his new ballet, *The Red Shoes*, composed by Julian Craster (Marius Goring) with whom she falls in love. Furious, jealous and uncompromising, Lermontov cruelly forces Vicky to choose between art and love, as her personal dilemma parallels the story of the ballet.

As Lermontov describes it, *The Ballet of the Red Shoes* is about a young girl who is devoured by an ambition to attend a dance in a pair of red shoes. She gets the shoes and goes to the Ball. For a time, all goes well, and she is happy. But at the end of the evening, she is tired and wants to go home. But the red shoes are not tired. The red shoes are never tired. They dance her out into the street; they dance her over the mountains and valleys, through fields and forests, through the night and day. Time rushes by, love rushes by, life rushes by, but the red shoes dance on.... In the end, she dies."

Red-haired Moira Shearer was a ballerina at Sadler's Welles, performing at Covent Garden, and the 20-minute ballet sequence utilized a corps de ballet of 53 dancers with music conducted by Sir. Thomas Beecham. Choreographer Robert Helpmann dances the part of the boyfriend with Leonide Massine creating his own choreography as the shoemaker.

Oscar-nominated for Best Picture, Best Screenplay. and Best Editing, it won two Academy Awards: Best Musical Score and Best Art-Set Decoration.

On the Granger Movie Gauge of 1 to 10, *The Red Shoes* is a dazzling yet tragic 10. Filmmakers Martin Scorsese and Brian De Palma cite it as one of their favorite films.

The Red Violin (Lions Gate Films) (1998)

Francois Girard's stirring, sumptuous epic follows the turbulent, if convoluted, journey of a legendary violin, famous for its perfect acoustics and unusual reddish hue. Up for auction in Canada, the stringed instrument has traveled around the globe for more than 300 years when an American expert (Samuel L. Jackson) is summoned to authenticate its worth.

Created by a 17th century Italian, Nicolo Bussotti (Carlo Cecchi), as a legacy of love for his unborn son, the violin becomes an embodiment of his grief when his beloved wife Anna (Irene Grazioli) and child die in childbirth. Mysteriously, a Tarot-card reader has predicted a long, nomadic, adventure-packed life for Anna, coupling her fate to the future "life" of the red violin.

As the intriguing story evolves, the spell of the violin seems to bewitch the lives of its various owners. It travels to monastic Austria, where it goes to a six-year-old child prodigy. In England, it falls into the decadent hands of a Byronic musician (Jason Flemyng) who uses it in his flamboyant courtship of a volatile novelist (Greta Scacchi).

From there, it's brought to Shanghai, where it winds up as a treasured artifact in the midst of the Chinese Cultural Revolution. Finally, Chinese authorities send it to the auction hall in modern-day Montreal, where eager bidders, descendants and friends of the people it has touched, are obsessed with acquiring the instrument. The mystery, of course, is who will wind up with this fabled masterpiece?

Although the pace and quality of the sprawling flashback episodes differ greatly, on the Granger Movie Gauge of 1 to 10, *The Red Violin* is an exquisite, captivating 9. It's a sweeping, cinematic symphony, a unique combination of classical and contemporary, both in music and imagery.

Remember (A24) (2015)

This unusual revenge story is unlike any other Holocaust-inspired movie you've ever seen!

Ninety-year-old Zev Guttman (Christopher Plummer) has dementia, so he's confused every morning when he awakens, calling for his wife Ruth. She's dead, but it takes him awhile to adjust to his memory loss.

Zev lives in a nursing home not far from New York, where his best friend is wheelchair-bound Max Rosenbaum (Martin Landau), who's hooked up to an oxygen tank.

They're both Auschwitz survivors, and Max has hatched a plan to wreak revenge on the sadistic guard who was responsible for tormenting and exterminating both of their families.

According to the Simon Wiesenthal Center, SS Officer Otto Wallisch escaped from Germany and has been living somewhere in North America under the assumed identity of Rudy Kurlander.

Having identified four elderly men with the name Rudy Kurlander, Max gives Zev a thick envelope filled with cash, train and bus tickets and an all-important letter detailing, step-by-step, his every move in a search to identify the culprit – and kill him.

Although Zev's distraught son (Henry Czerny) sends out a Missing Persons bulletin, Zev evades an F.B.I. background check when buying a Glock and slips, almost unnoticed, crossing into and out of Canada with an expired U.S. passport on his cross-country trek.

Scripted by newcomer Benjamin August, it's astutely directed by Canadian auteur Atom Egoyan (*The Sweet Hereafter, Where the Truth Lies*) with Jurgen Prochnow, Bruno Ganz, and Heinz Lieven as three of the four Rudys. Dean Norris is particularly effective as virulently anti-Semitic John Kurlander, a rural cop, the son of the deceased fourth Rudy, with a savage German Shepherd. Christopher Plummer's dignified, persuasive performance propels the Hitchcockian plot – with additional support from Peter DaCunha as a thoughtful youngster who befriends Zev on a Cleveland-bound train and Jane Spidell as the protective daughter of the last Kurlander on Zev's list.

On the Granger Movie Gauge of 1 to 10, *Remember* is an intriguing 8. It's an engaging Canadian import that should be on your "must see" list.

Robot & Frank
(Samuel Goldwyn/Stage 6) (2012)

Set in the near future, this sly, fanciful story revolves around Frank Weld (Frank Langella), an irascible, retired jewel thief, who is divorced and living alone in the old family house in rural Cold Spring, New York. The place is a slovenly mess and Frank's memory is obviously failing, which greatly concerns his grown children: exasperated Hunter (James Marsden) and peripatetic Madison (Liv Tyler) with whom he communicates via an advanced version of Skype.

Since Frank is adamant about not moving to a "memory facility," Hunter arrives one day with an electronic 'caregiver.' This expensive robot (voiced pitch-perfectly by Peter Sarsgaard) is specifically programmed to monitor Frank's daily activities in order to stimulate his mind and body, while making and serving him healthy, nourishing meals. At first Frank balks, but soon the cheerful robot is accompanying him everywhere, even to his favorite haunt, the local library.

That's where the kindly librarian Jennifer (Susan Sarandon) regretfully informs him that all the books are being removed to make way for the "digital experience." But locked in a safe, she's stashed a rare, valuable copy of *Don Quixote*, which Frank immediately plans to steal. To his surprise and delight, Frank discovers that, given proper instruction, robot learns how to pick locks quickly and, best of all, has no conscience. For the first time in his life, Frank has an accomplice, as one successful heist leads to another.

Making his feature film debut, commercial director Jake Schreier, working from a cleverly contrived script by Christopher Ford, establishes a light-hearted, believable bond between man and machine, even though robot repeatedly states that he does not have emotions.

In a tour-de-force performance, Frank Langella's crusty character not only has real memory lapses but can also feign them, like when he shoplifts at the chic boutique that's moved into the store front that was once his favorite café. This Alzheimer's allegory combines pathos with humor.

On the Granger Movie Gauge of 1 to 10, *Robot & Frank* is an amusing, ingratiating 8, leaving a bittersweet afterglow.

Royal Wedding (M.G.M.) (1951)

Inspired by the brother-and-sister dancing team of Fred and Adele Astaire and her subsequent marriage to Lord Charles Cavendish, son of the Duke of Devonshire, Alan Jay Lerner paired that idea with the real-life Royal Wedding of England's Queen Elizabeth II and Prince Philip.

So when the stars of Broadway's *Every Night at Seven*, Tom (Fred Astaire) and Ellen (Jane Powell) Bowen take their show to London in 1947 to capitalize on the imminent Royal Wedding, they both fall in love. Onboard ship, Ellen is smitten with aristocratic but impoverished Lord John Brindale (Peter Lawford), while Tom yearns for an engaged dancer, Anne Ashmond (Sarah Churchill). Complications arise and are conquered for a happy ending.

With Burton Lane's music and Alan Jay Lerner's lyrics, it's directed by Stanley Donen as part of the famed Arthur Freed production unit. What makes this particular 1951 musical memorable are two Astaire dance numbers: one with a coat rack in the ship's gym and another on the ceiling.

The trick behind Astaire's seemingly defying gravity was accomplished by placing a cube-shaped room within a steel cage which revolved 360 degrees. As the set rotated, he moved, along with the camera equipment and operator, who was strapped to the floor. This same technique was used to simulate zero gravity in *2001: A Space Odyssey*.

Although she's dazzlingly versatile, Jane Powell was not first choice. June Allyson was cast as Astaire's sister but she got pregnant. Then Judy Garland was chosen but her health was declining. Sarah Churchill had impressed Freed in a road company of *The Philadelphia Story* – and it helped that she was the daughter of Britain's Prime Minister Winston Churchill.

"How Could You Believe Me When I Said I Love You When You Know I've Been a Liar All My Life?" is considered the longest song title ever, while Astaire and Powell's comic vaudeville routine evokes memories of the "A Couple of Swells" number he did with Judy Garland in *Easter Parade*.

On the Granger Movie Gauge of 1 to 10, *Royal Wedding* is an imperial 8.

Saving Private Ryan (Paramount/ DreamWorks) (1998)

According to a *Variety* editor, Peter Bart's book *The Gross*: "The genesis of *Saving Private Ryan* can be traced directly to one studio executive's obsession. Don Granger, an executive vice-president of production at Paramount, was a man on a mission, and that mission was to add a movie about World War II to his studio's slate. 'Let's be honest about it,' he explained. 'One reason guys like me get into these jobs is that we were strongly influenced when we were growing up by a few special movies. And whether we realize it or not, we all are driven to remake these movies. In fact, we have this private conceit that we can make them better.'"

Don Granger is my son—and it was his concept that triggered Steven Spielberg's reinvention of the war movie genre. Screenwriter Robert Rodat's premise was simple: there were four Ryan brothers in combat during W.W. II; three had been killed and the War Department in Washington, D.C. was determined to bring home the last remaining brother. There were no superheroes, just a small group of soldiers sent on a mission they didn't completely believe in.

Photographed by Janusz Kaminsky, the first 24 minutes vividly chronicles the most brutal battle ever filmed as American troops land on Omaha Beach on June 6, 1944, known as D Day. Captain John Miller (Tom Hanks) and his Charlie Company, 2nd Ranger Battalion (Edward Burns, Vin Diesel, Adam Goldberg, Barry Pepper, Giovanni Ribisi and Tom Sizemore) are dispatched with a translator (Jeremy Davies) to locate Private James Ryan who parachuted into France the night before. Further complications arise when Pvt. Ryan (Matt Damon) refuses to return, insisting he has orders to continue fighting the Nazis who threaten a strategically important bridge over the Merderet River in the town of Ramelle.

Framed by a forward and epilogue, set in the American Cemetery and Memorial at Colleville-sur-mer in Normandy, Steven Spielberg's magnificent production garnered audience and critical acclaim – with 11 Academy Award nominations and Oscar wins for Directing, Cinematography, Editing, Sound and Sound Effects. The Omaha landing was voted the "best battle scene of all time" by Empire magazine and ranked #1 on TV Guide's list of the "50 Greatest Movie Moments."

On the Granger Movie Gauge of 1 to 10, *Saving Private Ryan* is a visceral, haunting, transformative 10, an epic war film.

The Sea Inside (Fine Line Features) (2004)

Compassionate euthanasia is the somber theme of this intelligent, insightful, internationally lauded Alejandro Amenabar melodrama from Spain that's fictional yet based on real-life events. In Spain's coastal Galicia region, quadriplegic Ramon Sampedro (Bardem) lies at home in bed, wryly begging to be put out of the helpless misery that he has endured for almost 30 years. Lovingly cared for by his stoic Celtic family, he spends years battling the Catholic Church and Spanish judicial system for the right to die with dignity.

To his aid come two women: a lawyer (Belen Rueda) who, although she too is suffering from a debilitating disease, helps Sampedro publish his first book and a lonely visitor (Lola Duenas), a naive single mother who gradually develops a deep understanding his plight. Both establish a romantic relationship with Ramon. Director and co-writer Amenabar (*The Others*) indulges in cinematic, even lyrical flights of fancy and copious symbolism while duly acknowledging the social implications of assisted suicide. But he and collaborator Mateo Gil never establish the profoundly essential emotional connection with his protagonist's quest to lift this film to greatness.

That's left entirely to the revelatory yet understated nuances of Javier Bardem (Oscar-nominated for *Before Night Falls*). The essential moral and ethical arguments of Ramon's choice to die are deliberately left unexplored.

A bizarre encounter with a quadriplegic priest, for example, is played for humor. If you're curious about the subject, Denys Arcand's *The Barbarian Invasions* is far more effective.

On the Granger Movie Gauge of 1 to 10, *The Sea Inside* is an agonizingly noble, mournful 7, primarily distinguished by Bardem's powerful, poignant performance.

The Secret of Roan Inish (First Look/ Columbia Tri-Star) (1994)

Based on Celtic folklore, this charming, cultural identity tale revolves around the legend of the "selkies," who are part/human, part/seal and can shed their sealskins and live on land.

It's shortly after W.W. II when 10 year-year-old Fiona Coneelly (Jeni Courtney) is sent by her widower father to live in a cottage with her grandparents in a fishing village near Donegal on Ireland's west coast - right across a sea channel from a tiny green island called Roan Inish, which, in Gaelic, means "island of the seals." Her maritime family had lived on Roan Inish for generations but they left during a tragic storm in which Fiona's baby brother, Jamie, was lost at sea in his wooden cradle. Or was he?

Always yearning for the sea, Fiona's grandfather Hugh (Mick Lally) recalls an ancestor who fought the British to defend the Irish language, while her God-fearing grandmother Tess (Eileen Colgan), knowing they may have to move further inland, laments, "To move off Roan Inish was bad enough, but to move out of sight of the sea…"

Further piquing Fiona's curiosity, her dark-eyed, dark-haired cousin Tadhg (John Lynch) explains how someone in the family - many years ago - fell in love with a beautiful "selkie" woman and fathered a brood with her before she found her sealskin where he'd hidden it, up under the roof, and returned to the sea in her marine mammal form.

The temptation to explore Roan Inish is more than Fiona can bear, so soon she's poking around the dilapidated huts and gardens, accompanied by her thirteen-year-old cousin, Eamon (Richard Sheridan). One day, when she sees a naked, dark-haired wild child picking flowers in a field, she calls out her brother's name, but the little boy quickly climbs into a tiny, boat-shaped cradle and paddles out to sea, accompanied by friendly seals. Was it Jamie?

Based on Rosalie K. Fry's novel, *The Secret of Ron Mor Skerry*and released in 1994, it was written and directed by independent filmmaker John Sayles (*Return of the Secaucus Seven, Eight Men Out, Passion Fish*). Magnificently photographed by Haskell Wexler on Ireland's rugged northwest seacoast and accompanied by a lilting Celtic soundtrack, it's more of an allegorical meditation or magical tone poem.

On the Granger Movie Gauge of 1 to 10, *The Secret of Roan Inish* is an authentic, indelible, idiomatic 9—no blarney.

A Separation
(Sony Pictures Classics) (2011)

Acclaimed as one of the best foreign films of 2011, writer/director Asghar Farhadi's meditation on marital conflict is set in contemporary Iran, where two couples are dragged before a judge to defend themselves and their legal, moral and religious beliefs in a family court.

As the drama begins, after a year-and-a-half of bureaucratic aggravation, Simin (Leila Hatami) has finally received permission for her family to emigrate from urban Tehran and is trying to convince her secular, banker husband Nader (Peyman Moadi) and adolescent daughter Termeh (played by the director's daughter, Sarina Farhadi) to opt for a better life. But middle-class, moderate Nader feels he must stay to care for his frail father (Ali-Asghar Shahbazi) who is afflicted with Alzheimer's. So when frustrated Simin, who is a doctor, moves back to her parents' home, Nader hires poor, pious Razieh (Sareh Bayet) to take care of his father during the day, unbeknownst to her debt-ridden, unemployed husband, Hodjat (Shahab Hosseni).

When pregnant Razieh is subsequently injured in a tragic accident, the foursome winds up before an Iranian judge and, eventually, it's up to confused yet intuitive, eleven-year-old Termeh to decide what her future will be.

Filled with ethical and cultural issues about the condition of women in Iran, the script is complicated and somewhat confusing unless one is familiar with the Islamic theocracy that has dominated Iran's 70 million people since the 1979 revolution. But the human condition it depicts is universal, and it's not difficult to identify with the deceits and philosophical dilemma faced by each of the characters.

"As Ingmar Bergman used to say, messages are for the telegraph office," Asghar Farhadi (*About Elly*) told interviews. "There's a difference between intention and messages. My intention was to create a story and let you interpret what it means. To me, that is more effective filmmaking than to just give a manifesto or slogans."

In Persian with English subtitles, on the Granger Movie Gauge of 1 to 10, *A Separation* is an ambiguous, enigmatic 8, revolving around the termination of a marriage.

Seven Brides for Seven Brothers (M.G.M.) (1954)

Most memorable for its innovative choreography, this musical was a 1954 Best Picture Oscar nominee and also won an Academy Award for its score by Saul Chaplin, Gene de Paul, and Johnny Mercer. Set in 1850 in the Oregon Territory, the plot is lifted from Plutarch's tale about early Romans who stole women from the neighboring Sabine tribe in order to propagate and multiply. Only, this time, the instigator is Adam Pontipee (Howard Keel) who brings his bride Milly (Jane Powell) to his cabin in the mountains, where she discovers that Adam is the oldest of seven rowdy brothers for whom she'll have to cook and clean. Named alphabetically from the Old Testament, there's Adam, Benjamin, Caleb, Daniel, Ephraim, Frank (short for Frankincense) and Gideon.

After Milly teaches them manners, the brothers attend a barn-raising, where they flirt with six girls. While the Pontipees aren't to blame for the ensuing brawl, they're banned from town. Lovelorn and lonely, they decide to adopt Plutarch's idea and kidnap the women they're pining for, creating an avalanche so they cannot be followed. Furious that they forgot to bring a preacher along, Milly dispatches the brothers to the barn while the girls live in the house, and indignant Adam opts to spend the winter alone in a trapping hut. As months pass, the girls gradually fall in love with the brothers and Milly gives birth to a daughter, Hannah. But, come spring, it's inevitable that the townspeople will clamor for revenge.

Director Stanley Donen (*Royal Wedding, Singin' in the Rain*) often said he wished he'd been able to shoot the picture on location in Oregon and not have to rely on phony painted backgrounds but instead M.G.M. spent a big part of the budget creating two versions so all theaters could screen it.

Choreographer Michel Kidd cast trained dancers as the frontiersman, including Jacques d'Amboise from the New York City Ballet, and Julie Newmar (billed as "Newmeyer") can be glimpsed as the partner of former baseball player Jeff Richards. Costume designer Walter Plunkett fashioned the girls' dresses from old quilts that he'd found at the Salvation Army.

Jane Powell recalls that, during filming, dancer Jacques d'Amboise was very shy and didn't talk much, leading her to assume that, because his name was French, he didn't speak much English: "It wasn't until I moved to New York and we met again that I realized he doesn't speak French at all. He's not only an American but he has a distinctive New York accent."

On the Granger Movie Gauge of 1 to 10, *Seven Brides for Seven Brothers* is a tuneful 10, bearing a recommendation from then-President Dwight D. Eisenhower, saying, "If you haven't seen it, you should see it."

The Silence of the Lambs (Orion Pictures) (1991)

Considered to be the first gruesome horror picture to win the Academy Award as Best Picture, this chilling 1991 crime thriller introduces brilliant psychiatrist Hannibal Lecter as an enigmatic, cannibalistic serial killer.

It begins as a young FBI trainee, Clarice Starling (Jodie Foster), is sent to Baltimore State Hospital for the Criminally Insane to interview prisoner Hannibal Lecter (Anthony Hopkins) to find out what he knows about a serial killer nicknamed "Buffalo Bill" (Ted Levine), who skins his female victims' corpses. A U.S. Senator's daughter, Catherine Martin (Brooke Smith), has been kidnapped by him, and senior agent Jack Crawford (Scott Glenn) of the Bureau's Behavioral Science Unit authorizes her to offer Lecter a fake prison transfer deal if his information helps to rescue the young woman. That ignites a dark, demonically morbid mind game between strong, smart Starling and sadistic, diabolically manipulative Lecter.

Adapted by Ted Tally from Thomas Harris' best-seller and directed by Jonathan Demme, it's filled with deliciously decadent dialogue, like when Lecter teasingly taunts Clarice with" "A census taker once tried to test me. I ate his liver with some fava beans and nice Chianti."

Hannibal Lecter was first introduced as a secondary character in Thomas Harris' *Red Dragon*, which was first filmed under the title *Manhunter* (1986) with Brian Cox as the demented doctor. Although other actors have been cast as Lecter in subsequent, lesser films, Anthony Hopkins has made the creepy, charismatic role indelibly his own. Curiously, neither Hopkins nor Foster was Jonathan Demme's first choice for their respective roles; Sean Connery turned him down, as did Michelle Pfeiffer.

Although this was only the third film in Oscar history to sweep all five major awards (Best Picture, Best Director, Best Actor. Best Actress and Best Adapted Screenplay), Orion Pictures went bankrupt the following year due to its disastrous television ventures.

The 2007 DVD Collector's Edition, includes several deleted scenes and Hannibal Lecter's phone greetings, along with Thomas Harris' real-life inspiration for the ghoulish killer, including Ted Tally's revelatory admission about Buffalo Bill's homosexuality: "We certainly wish we'd crafted that character in some different way. At least, God forbid, not given him a white poodle that he names Precious."

On the Granger Movie Gauge of 1 to 10, *The Silence of the Lambs* is a suspenseful, terrifying 10. It's a malevolent masterpiece.

Singin' in the Rain (M.G.M.) (1952)

Nacio Herb Brown's song *Singin' in the Rain* has been featured in many musicals since 1929, but no interpretation has been as iconic as Gene Kelly's umbrella-twirling, puddle-splashing version in this 1952 film. Utilizing a witty script by Betty Comden and Adolph Green, lyricist-turned-producer Arthur Freed and co-directors Stanley Donen and Gene Kelly whimsically satirized Hollywood's transition from silent films to "talkies."

Having completed *An American in Paris*, Gene Kelly was at the peak of his career as Monumental Pictures' swashbuckling idol Don Lockwood - with Donald O'Connor as Cosmo, his piano-playing partner. Jean Hagen was cast as ditzy, vapid Lina Lamont, and then-newcomer Debbie Reynolds snagged the part of Kathy Selden, the chorus girl Gene falls in love with.

Turning the clock back was easier said than done, according to art directors Randall Duell and Cedric Gibbons, set decorator Jacques Mapes and costumer Walter Plunkett, who spent months tracking down flapper clothes and recording equipment that had been dispatched to museums. The car Debbie drives at the beginning of the film was actually Andy Hardy's old jalopy.

Kelly's rain-drenched scene with the lamppost was shot on the Culver City lot's "East Side Street," where chalk marks indicated where puddles were to be formed; even though Kelly was sick with a 103 fever, it took just two days to film.

Pivotal to the plot is Reynolds' dubbing Lina Lamont's squawky voice, but—in reality—Debbie's voice was dubbed by uncredited Betty Noyes, and Jean Hagen, using her normal voice, dubbed Debbie's lines for the scenes in which Debbie was supposed to be her. Lina Lamont's character is supposedly based on Norma Talmadge, who couldn't make the transition to "talkies," and Rita Moreno's Zelda Zanders, Lina's informant friend and the "Zip Girl," was Clara Bow.

Singin' in the Rain garnered only two Academy Award nominations, one for its musical score and one for comedic Jean Hagen. If Oscar voters were unimpressed, audiences were – and continue to flock to this perennial favorite. Kelly's title song sequence opens The Great Movie Ride at Disney's Hollywood Studios in Orlando, Florida – and he, personally, approved the audio-animatronics.

On the Granger Movie Gauge of 1 to 10, *Singin' in the Rain* is a tuneful 10 —matching its 10 musical numbers, including *All I Do Is Dream of You, Make 'Em Laugh, You Were Meant for Me, You Are My Lucky Star, Moses Supposes*, and *Good Morning*.

Slumdog Millionaire (Fox Searchlight/ Warner Bros.) (2008)

When eighteen-year-old Jamal Malik (Dev Patel) from the streets of Mumbai comes up with an unlikely stream of correct answers, winning millions of rupees on India's version of *Who Wants to Be a Millionaire*, he's suspected of cheating by the game show's host (Anil Kapoor). Grilled by a police investigator (Irrfan Khan), Jamal reluctantly reveals how his intricate, Dickensian life experiences have informed his knowledge. As a child, sensitive Jamal and his older brother, Salim, were left to fend for themselves in the squalid slums when their mother was killed in a mob attack on Muslims.

At Jamal's insistence, they take in a third urchin, a girl named Latika, envisioning themselves as the Three Musketeers. After they're captured by a vicious, Fagin-like operator who trains street beggars, crafty Salim saves Jamal from mutilation. But as they escape by jumping on a moving train, they're separated from Latika, whom Jamal loves.

In a hilarious sequence, the boys find themselves at the Taj Mahal, where they pose as guides, dispensing misinformation and scamming gullible tourists. Eventually, Salim (Madhur Mittal) falls in with gangsters, while Jamal toils as a lowly tea-server at XL5 Communications and is determined to 'rescue' Latika (Freida Pinto).

Working with screenwriter Simon Beaufoy (*The Full Monty*), adapting Vikas Swarup's novel *Q&A*, Danny Boyle (*Trainspotting, Millions, 28 Days Later*) skillfully concocts in flashback an ironic, vividly irresistible saga of courage and determination, introducing an exotic socio-economic-cultural angle which makes this premise fresh and filled with unexpected moments of revelation.

Add the vibrant cinematography and kinetic energy of the throbbing soundtrack and on the Granger Movie Gauge of 1 to 10, *Slumdog Millionaire* is an intoxicating, triumphant 10. Brutal and beautiful, tragic and joyful, it's one of the year's best movies, a must-see!

Snowpiercer (The Weinstein Company) (2013)

South Korean Filmmaker Bong Joon-ho's first English-language production is a bold, compelling, fantastical action thriller.

When global warming was finally acknowledged as a worldwide threat, scientists sent a missile into space to lower Earth's thermostat. Instead, the device triggered another Ice Age, killing everyone except those who managed to get onboard an immense bullet train that's been circling the glacial planet for 17 years.

Passengers are strictly segregated by class, and compartmentalized order within the convoy is ruthlessly enforced by a grotesquely fascistic bureaucrat (Tilda Swinton) with her armed guards. When one of the impoverished dares to complain, his arm is inserted into a porthole, frozen and amputated. But rebellion is brewing in the slums in the back of the train, where restless Curtis (bearded Chris Evans, a.k.a. *Captain America*), encouraged by elderly, peg-legged Gilliam (John Hurt), decides to lead a guerrilla force to the front, where the train's quasi-mythical inventor, enigmatic Mr. Wilford (Ed Harris) rules in *Wizard-of-Oz*-like mystery from the engine room.

Accompanied by his loyal friend Edgar (Jamie Bell) and a determined mother (Olivia Spencer) whose child has been abducted, Curtis bribes a drug-addicted security expert (Song Kang-ho) and his drug-dazed daughter/apprentice (Ko Ah-sung) to open the locked 'gates' separating the railway cars by giving them Kronole, the hallucinogen they crave. As the insurgents move forward car-by-car, examining the self-sustaining ecosystem, one of their more memorable encounters is with a creepily cheerful schoolmarm (Alison Pill), another depicts the various luxuries enjoyed by the elite.

Based on a 1982 French graphic novel, *La Transperceneige*, it's propelled by Bong Joon-ho's imaginative visuality and gripping suspense, which more than compensate for the heavy-handed, dystopian allegory.

Filmed on gimbals on interconnected soundstages at Prague's Barrandov Studios in the Czech Republic for an astonishing $40 million, it's not been widely distributed because Harvey Weinstein reportedly wanted to edit out 20 minutes and Bong refused.

On the Granger Movie Gauge of 1 to 10, *Snowpiercer* hurtles by with an exciting, edge-of-your-seat 8 – a wild ride that's one of the best of the year, so far.

The Social Network (Columbia Pictures) (2010)

Microsoft visionary Bill Gates once said, "As we look ahead into the next century, leaders will be those who empower others." And that's why this astute tale about brilliant Facebook co-founder/CEO Mark Zuckerberg is so fascinating.

Cleverly adapted by witty Aaron Sorkin (*The West Wing, Charlie Wilson's War*) from Ben Mezrich's non-fiction best-seller "The Accidental Billionaire," perceptively cast and inventively directed by David Fincher (*The Curious Case of Benjamin Button, Zodiac, Fight Club*), the compelling drama centers on a contentious courtroom conflict between frustrated twenty-six-year-old Zuckerberg and three of his Harvard cohorts over ownership of the Facebook idea.

Like *Rashomon*, each justifies and validates in his contradictory deposition his recollection about how it all began and grew into a worldwide, culturally defining phenomenon.

From the first insightful scene, set in the fall of 2003, it's obvious that brash, neurotic, socially inept Mark Zuckerberg (Jesse Eisenberg) yearns for acceptance.

Dumped by his girlfriend, Erica Albright (Rooney Mara), he drunkenly hacks into the university's computers to trash her on-line and creates FaceMash, in which two women's photographs are displayed and viewers are urged to choose which is "hotter." Face Mash instantly goes viral, crashing the system, but not before it's noticed by two upperclassmen, the WASPy uber-entitled Winklevoss twins (Armie Hammer, Josh Pence), who recruit him to design a Harvard dating website. But Zuckerberg thinks bigger and, bankrolled by his Brazilian-born best-friend/roommate Eduardo Saverin (Andrew Garfield), invents Facebook.

Then ruthless Napster entrepreneur Sean Parker (Justin Timberlake) diabolically comes on the scene, bringing in investors to elevate and, perhaps, exploit the fledgling phenomenon to an astonishing level. (If Facebook were a nation, it would now be the third largest country in the world, more than 1.5 times as populous as the United States.)

While the Facebook communication concept revolves around computer technology, the enthralling story it has spawned delves into humanity to the core, involving loneliness, loyalty, friendship, greed, envy and betrayal.

On the Granger Movie Gauge of 1 to 10, *The Social Network* is a provocative, tantalizing 10, never quite delineating the truth.

Some Like It Hot (United Artists: MGM/UA) (1959)

O f all the sophisticated European writers, directors and producers who fled Hitler and enriched American movies, Billy Wilder was perhaps the most successful. Teaching himself English by listening to the radio and learning 10 new words daily, he was, above all, a story-teller. His corrosive wit and acrid dialogue merged pessimistic German expressionism with the American crime drama in this romantic screwball comedy, released in 1959.

Joe (Tony Curtis) and Jerry (Jack Lemmon) are two Chicago musicians who inadvertently witness the St. Valentine's Day Massacre. Spotted by the gangland killers as they flee from the scene of the crime, they go on the lam masquerading as women in an all-female band. Problem is: Joe falls for the singer Sugar Kane (Marilyn Monroe), while Jerry is ardently pursued by an amorous millionaire yachtsman (Joe E. Brown). Yet neither can reveal his true gender because the mobsters are on their trail.

This first film co-authored by Wilder and I.A.L. Diamond is based on a 1935 French movie musical, *Fanfare d'Amour*, written by Robert Thoeren and Michael Logan, which was remade in 1951 by German director Kurt Hoffmann as *Fanfaren der Liebe*. However, in the European versions, there's no gangster subplot.

Under Billy Wilder's deft direction, broad slapstick is offset by sly sexual innuendos. And he correctly gauged the acceptance of two heterosexual men who reluctantly cross-dress reluctantly but end up discovering entirely new facets of their personalities and developing a greater sensitivity toward women.

Although she was perennially late on the set and often unable to learn her lines, Marilyn Monroe was paid $100,000 plus a historic 10% of the gross profits. Originally, Wilder wanted to cast Mitzi Gaynor with Bob Hope and Danny Kaye as the leads, but he was delighted with Lemmon and Curtis.

Nominated for Academy Awards in six categories, it won only one Oscar, bestowed on Orry-Kelly for Best Costume Design. Nevertheless, it spawned Gower Champion's 1972 Broadway musical *Sugar*. In 2000, the American Film Institute named it the greatest American comedy of all time.

On the Granger Movie Gauge of 1 to 10, *Some Like It Hot* is an uninhibited, antic 10, concluding with what is arguably the funniest final line in motion picture history: when Jack Lemmon reveals to besotted Joe E. Brown that he's really a man, Brown philosophically responds, "Nobody's perfect."

Somewhere in Time (Universal Pictures) (1980)

After achieving worldwide acclaim as *Superman* (1978), Christopher Reeve chose to play Richard Collier in Richard Matheson's screen adaptation of his sci-fi novel *Bid Time Return*. Inspired by photograph of early 20th century stage actress Maude Adams, Matheson devised a story about a man who became so obsessed by the portrait of a woman that he travels back in time to meet her.

Beginning at the Grand Hotel on Mackinac Island, Michigan, a sensitive, contemporary Chicago playwright Collier becomes transfixed by a radiant 1912 photograph of stage actress Elise McKenna (Jane Seymour). By sheer force of will, he goes back into the past, where his attempts to woo McKenna are repeatedly thwarted by her Svengali-like manager (Christopher Plummer).

After reading Matheson's novel, my brother Stephen Deutsch (who later changed his name back to Simon to honor our biological father, S Sylvan Simon) vowed film it, engaging Jeannot Szwarc (*Jaws II*) to direct it. Released in October, 1980, the film was trashed by critics and received its only Academy Award nomination for Best Costume Design.

Astoundingly, it was resurrected on cable television, where it achieved immense popularity, followed by steadily climbing video sales. In 1984, when it was released in Hong Kong, it rose to rank 6th in the Top 10 Highest Grossing Films of all time in China.

There's a strong parallel between Matheson's story and Jack Finney's novel *Time and Again*, acknowledged in homage as the professor whom Collier consults about time travel is named Finney. And John Barry's haunting musical score encompasses the 18th variation of Sergei Rachmaninoff's "Rhapsody on a Theme of Paganini."

Built in 1887, The Grand Hotel held its first "SIT" weekend in 1991, inaugurating what has become a sold-out seasonal event. No automobiles are allowed on Macinkac Island, where everyone, including cast and crew, traveled to and from the set on bicycles.

In his 1998 autobiography, *Still Me*, Christopher Reeve recalled, "The real world fell away as the story and the setting took hold of us. I've rarely worked on a production that was so relaxed and harmonious. Even the hard-boiled Teamsters and grips from Chicago succumbed to the charms of the island and the mellow atmosphere on the set."

On the Granger Movie Gauge of 1 to 10, *Somewhere in Time* is an enduring fantasy 10, a romantic cult classic that transcends space and time.

Son of Saul (Sony Pictures Classics) (2015)

Set in the Auschwitz-Birkenau death camp in October, 1944, this powerful, poignant story revolves around a Hungarian Jewish prisoner named Saul Auslander (Geza Rohrig). He's a member of the Sonderkommando, a group of prisoners assigned the grim task of carrying corpses from the gas chamber to the crematorium, then carting away the ashes to be discarded.

As Allied Forces draw closer to the camp, the pace of killing is accelerated. Among the dead, Saul finds the body of a young boy he claims as his son, and he becomes obsessed with finding a rabbi among the prisoners to say Kaddish (the prayer for the dead) and give the child a proper burial.

Inspired by *Voices from Beneath the Ashes*, true tales from Auschwitz which was published in Jean-Paul Sartre's periodical *Les Temps Modernes*, Hungarian-born writer/director Laszlo Nemes noted: "The story of the Holocaust is not the story of the exceptions who survived. It is the story of the dead."

Co-scripting with Clara Royer, first-time feature film director Nemes reveals the agony solely through Saul's perception, as cinematographer Matyas Erdely consigns violence and nudity into the un-focused background, along with the desperate wailing and persistent screaming. Adding to the chilling effect, there is no musical score.

As a former watchmaker-turned locksmith, Saul's urgency is further heightened by plans for an upcoming Sonderkommando rebellion and their interaction with SS guards and Oberkapos (superior officers).

"You've failed the living to help the dead," he's told.

So add *Son of Saul* to the pantheon of visceral, visually striking Holocaust films that includes *Schindler's List, Shoah, The Grey Zone,* and *Life is Beautiful.*

In Hungarian, Yiddish, German, and Polish with English subtitles, *Son of Saul* is an intense, engrossing 8, an existential warning from history—and Hungary's Official Selection for the Academy Award as Best Foreign Language Film.

Space Cowboys (Warner Bros.) (2000)

In a season of admittedly disappointing features, now there's a terrific reason to orbit the box-office: Team Daedalus. Back in 1958, they were the bravest, boldest, fastest Air Force test pilots—until they were grounded so that NASA could send a chimpanzee into space.

Now, 42 years later, the Russian satellite Ikon has suffered a systems failure that the Russians insist will cause a total communications blackout. Since Ikon has the same guidance system as an early American Skylab, its designer, played by Clint Eastwood, should know how to repair the antiquated technology. Only, he won't go into space without the only crew he trusts: fearless pilot Tommy Lee Jones, astrophysicist/ladies' man Donald Sutherland and robotics expert turned Baptist preacher James Garner. But first these geriatric hotshots have to get through training and fulfill the physical requirements for spaceflight. Because of the buddies' humorous bantering, this part is hilarious.

Even the obvious clichés seem to have a fresh spin. Then the countdown comes and the real challenge begins. Written by Ken Kaufman & Howard Klausner and directed by Clint Eastwood, each character's strengths and weaknesses are so well delineated that you have an emotional investment in their success – and survival.

After a slow start, the first two-thirds of the story is light-hearted, while the final third is suspenseful and serious. There's nothing but class and quality in this wonderfully performed production, a high-tech action-adventure that's perfect for family viewing.

On the Granger Movie Gauge of 1 to 10, *Space Cowboys* blasts off with an irresistibly exciting, adventurous 8. "Fun" is the operative word for this crowd-pleaser.

Spotlight (Open Road) (2015)

Best Picture at the 2016 Oscars, this is the fascinating, true crime story of the Pulitzer Prize-winning Boston Globe investigation that revealed the Roman Catholic Church's systematic 'cover-up' of pedophile priests.

Spotlight is the name of the Globe's investigative team, headed by Walter "Robby" Robinson (Michael Keaton) and comprised of Michael Rezendes (Mark Ruffalo), Sarah Pfeiffer (Rachel McAdams) and Matty Carroll (Brian d'Arcy James). They report to managing editor Ben Bradlee, Jr. (John Slattery), whose father figured prominently in the Watergate-themed *All the President's Men*.

After the Globe was bought by the New York Times in 2001, there's a new, cost-cutting boss, Marty Baron (Liev Schrieber), who is not only Jewish but also an out-of-towner. He fearlessly urges them to pursue molestation allegations against a single priest, a subject the newspaper has traditionally ignored under tacit pressure from Cardinal Bernard Law (Len Cariou) and officials in the Archdiocese of Boston.

Spotlight soon learns that it's not an isolated incident. Indeed, scores of similar claims have been privately settled by the Church's evasive attorney, Eric MacLeish (Billy Crudup), outside of the legal system, and those involving paperwork have been sealed by complicit judges. Thereby "turning child abuse into a cottage industry."

Scripted as a fact-based, journalistic procedural by Josh Singer (*The Fifth Estate*) and director Tom McCarthy (*The Station Agent, Win Win*), it reveals the institutional conspiracy that protected these predators and perpetuated their heinous behavior, moving them from parish to parish.

Unfortunately, that doesn't allow for much character development on the part of the Spotlight team, who doggedly pursue leads and interview victims and parishioners who are willing to talk. A notable exception is testy Mitchell Garabedian (Stanley Tucci), who steers them in the right direction when he realizes their serious intent.

Nevertheless, the entire ensemble scores—delivering solid performances.

On the Granger Movie Gauge of 1 to 10, *Spotlight* is a taut, compelling 10, illuminating a timely, still-relevant issue.

Star Trek (Paramount Pictures) (2009)

Forty-two-year-old director J.J. Abrams, creator of TV's *Alias* and *Lost,* has done the impossible: not only resurrected Gene Roddenberry's forty-three-year-old *Star Trek* franchise, a concept that was built on space-age idealism, but also re-imagined it for cynical 21st century moviegoers.

Utilizing an ingenious 'alternate reality' device and a bit of time-travel by Leonard Nimoy (the only original cast member to appear), it explores the backstory of the U.S.S. Enterprise crew. There's reckless, self-assured James Tiberius Kirk (Chris Pine from *Princess Diary 2*), sneaking aboard the departing USS Enterprise starship on its maiden voyage with his wry buddy, Dr. Leonard "Bones" McCoy (Karl Urban from *The Bourne Supremacy*), after matching wits at Starfleet Academy with the half-Vulcan/half-human Spock (Zachary Quinto from *Heroes*). He's has already caught the amorous eye of seductive Uhura (Zoe Saldana from *Drumline*), the alert communications officer who picks up and translates the distress call that summons them to their new adventure: trying to thwart the wrath of Nero (Eric Bana from *Troy* and *Munich*), the Romulan villain determine to wreak revenge for a horrific disaster that has yet to happen.

On the bridge is pilot Hikaru Sulu (John Cho from *American Pie*) with navigator Pavel Chekov (Anton Yelchin from *Alpha Dog* via Leningrad). And in the midst of battle, ingenious engineer Montgomery Scott (British comedian Simon Pegg from *Shaun of the Dead*) beams up, deciding, "I like this ship. It's exciting!" He's right.

Thanks to J.J. Abrams and screenwriters Alex Kurtzman and Roberto Orci, there are a number of subtle references to "Trek" history, like the appearance of stoic Capt. Christopher Pike (Bruce Greenwood) and McCoy's disclaimer, "I'm a doctor, not a physicist," and sputtering to Spock, "Are you out of your Vulcan mind?" But if you've never traveled at warp speed before, it doesn't matter because the heart and humor are there.

On the Granger Movie Gauge of 1 to 10, *Star Trek* boldly blasts off with a terrific 10 and warps into a new galaxy of entertaining sci-fi adventure.

Star Wars Film Series (20th Century-Fox) (1977-2005)

In hindsight, it's hard to believe that several studios passed on *Star Wars* before Alan Ladd Jr., head of production at 20th Century-Fox, decided to gamble on George Lucas's mythology for the space age.

Lucas's epic, set "a long time ago in a galaxy far, far away" dispatches the young hero Luke Skywalker (Mark Hamill), his mystical Jedi teacher Obi-Wan Kenobi (Alec Guinness) and wizened mentor Yoda, along with mercenary Han Solo (Harrison Ford), his towering Wookie companion Chewbacca (Peter Mayhew) and two "droids" – C3PO and R2D2 – to rescue Princess Leia (Carrie Fisher), the rebel leader of her planet, from the clutches of the evil Empire that's embodied by its helmeted enforcer Darth Vader (David Prowse, voiced by James Earl Jones).

The first trilogy tells the story of Luke Skywalker and Princess Leia, while the second trilogy is a prequel, focusing on their Jedi warrior father, Anakin Skywalker (Hayden Christensen), his love for Queen Padme Amidala (Natalie Portman), and fall from grace to become Darth Vader. One of the prominent elements is the "Force," an omnipresent energy that can be harnessed by those with a special ability; the Jedi use the Force for good, and the Sith use the dark side for evil. For inspiration, Lucas drew from many major religions, including Christianity, Buddhism, and Hinduism.

While Lucas revolutionized the concept of computerized special effects through Industrial Light & Magic, he utilized the droids, the spaceship, the alien entities, and the battles as background for the human drama that unfolds over the course of six films, covering a variety of genres, including science-fiction, the Western, the war film and the quasi-mystical epic.

Along with *Jaws, Star Wars* initiated the seismic tradition of the summer entertainment blockbuster or 'tent pole' feature that would open on many screens at the same time, launching profitable merchandising tie-in franchises.

When U.S. President Ronald Reagan proposed the Strategic Defense Initiative (SDI) to intercept incoming ICBMs, the plan was labeled *Star Wars*, as Reagan described the Soviet Union as an "evil empire." Later, the Smithsonian's National Air and Space Museum in Washington, D.C. had an exhibition called "Star Wars: The Magic of Myth," showing production models, props and character costumes, and in 2007, NASA launched a space shuttle carrying one of Lucas's original lightsabers into orbit.

On the Granger Movie Gauge of 1 to 10, *Star Wars* is a resonant, visionary 10, becoming a pop culture phenomenon that has not only permeated our consciousness but awakened wondrous childhood memories in countless adults.

Star Wars: The Force Awakens (Disney) (2015)

Writer/director J.J. Abrams has successfully revived George Lucas's original sci-fi concept, a space Western that captivated global audiences some 30+ years ago, bringing back Han Solo (Harrison Ford), Princess Leia (Carrie Fisher), Luke Skywalker (Mark Hamill), Chewbacca (Peter Mayhew), R2-D2 (Kenny Baker) and C-3PO (Anthony Daniels).

It opens with John Williams' familiar musical fanfare, along with that rolling scroll, explaining that Luke Skywalker has disappeared and the evil First Order has taken power. Enter Stormtroopers, led by Kylo Ren (Adam Driver), whose black mask and cape make him look just like Darth Vader. They're searching for a map that can lead them to where Luke is hiding; it's is hidden within spherical droid BB-8 that belongs to hotshot pilot Poe Dameron (Oscar Isaac).

When conscience-stricken Stormtrooper FN-3182, nicknamed Finn (John Boyega), defects, he joins up with Poe and Rey (Daisy Ridley), the feisty Jakku desert 'scavenger' who is protecting BB-8, as they steal an aged freighter, the Millennium Falcon, belonging to legendary smuggler Han Solo.

"Are you really Han Solo?"

"I used to be," he answers gruffly, obviously preferring the company of his Wookiee co-pilot, Chewbacca.

So they're off to find the Resistance, led by a now overseeing General Leia – and more than that I don't want to tell you.

As the narrative unfolds, new characters are seamlessly melded with old ones, particularly wizened, goggles-wearing, bar-owner Maz Kanata (motion-captured by Lupita Nyong'o), evoking memories of Jedi Yoda, and a hologram of the First Order's Supreme Leader Snoke (motion-captured by Andy Serkis).

Working with co-writers Lawrence Kasdan and Michael Arndt, J.J. Abrams continues Lucas's thematic, Joseph Campbell-inspired mythology, adding fast-paced twists and tragic turns, along with startling character revelations, amplified by exciting battle sequences and visual effects.

FYI: George Lucas sold his franchise for $4 billion to the Walt Disney Company in 2012. And Carrie Fisher's daughter, Billie Lourd (TV's *Scream Queens*), does a cameo as Leia's lieutenant.

On the Granger Movie Gauge of 1 to 10, *Star Wars: The Force Awakens* is a thrilling 10, marking a rebirth in exciting galactic entertainment!

State Fair (20th Century-Fox) (1945)

Depicting quintessential Midwestern Americana during the mid-20th century, *State Fair* is the only Rodgers and Hammerstein musical written directly for film.

As the amiable Frake family leaves their Brunswick farm for their annual trip to the Iowa State Fair, their heads are filled with hopes and dreams. Father Abel (Charles Winninger) anticipates that his beloved boar, Blue Boy, will win a top prize. Mother Melissa (Fay Bainter) hopes that her homemade pickles and mincemeat will triumph over her perennial rival's. Son Wayne (Dick Haymes) is determined to teach a lesson to one of the carnival barkers (Harry Morgan), and Margy (Jeanne Crain) just yearns for something to lift her melancholy spirits.

After settling into their trailer on the fairgrounds, Margy meets Des Moines Register newspaper writer Pat Gilbert (Dana Andrews), while Wayne is smitten by band singer Emily Edwards (Vivian Blaine) – and veteran character actors like Percy Kilbride, Frank McHugh and Donald Meek are scene-stealers.

Based on the Philip Strong novel, it was originally adapted by Sonya Levien and Paul Green for a 1933 comedy with Will Rogers and Louise Dresser. This time, it was scripted by Oscar Hammerstein II and Richard Rodgers, who propel the plot with songs like "It's A Grand Night for Singing," "Our State Fair," "That's for Me," "Isn't It Kind of Fun?" and "All I Owe Ioway." The poignant "It Might as Well Be Spring" won the 1945 Academy Award for Best Song.

While Dick Haymes and Vivian Blaine were well known '40s crooners, Jeanne Crain's singing voice was dubbed by Louanne Hogan. Crain, nevertheless, became a popular movie star, later winning an Oscar nomination for the title role in Elia Kazan's *Pinky*.

Jose Ferrer ineptly remade *State Fair* in 1962 with Pat Boone and Ann-Margret and, in 1996, it became a Broadway musical with additional songs lifted from other Rodgers and Hammerstein scores.

On the Granger Movie Gauge of 1 to 10, *State Fair* is a nostalgic, entrancing 8. When compared with M.G.M. movie musicals, this Fox feature, directed by Walter Lang, is, perhaps, not one of Hollywood's finest, but I saw it when I was a child and was absolutely spellbound. Growing up in Beverly Hills, I never knew any farm families and going to a real State Fair was a fantasy I cherished until I was an adult. Watching *State Fair* still makes me profoundly happy.

Sullivan's Travels (Paramount Pictures) (1941)

Known as the first major screenwriter to cross over into directing, Preston Sturges is often cited for his flamboyant screwball comedies, like *The Great McGinty, Christmas in July,* and *The Lady Eve.* But *Sullivan's Travels* (1941) is an irreverently funny, exquisitely paced, genre-crossing trip through Hollywood's dream factory that purposefully detours through the poverty-stricken streets of post-Depression America.

Opening with "To the memory of those who made us laugh: the motley mountebanks, the clowns, the buffoons, in all times and in all nations, whose efforts have lightened our burden a little, this picture is affectionately dedicated."

Idealistic John L. Sullivan (Joel McCrea) is a successful movie director who's become tired of making shallow comedies and musicals, telling his stunned studio boss that he wants his next project to be a socially significant drama based on Sinclair Beckstein's novel, *O Brother, Where Art Thou?*

Earnestly determined to "know trouble" first-hand, through the struggles and plight of the common man, Sullivan sets out on the open road disguised as a penniless hobo. At a diner, he meets The Girl (Veronica Lake), a discouraged young actress who becomes his traveling companion. Complications arise, not the least of which is Sullivan's loveless marriage, and danger lurks as he's knocked unconscious, thrown into the boxcar of a freight train, implicated in a murder and sentenced to serve six years on a chain gang. Yet in the depths of hardship and bleak despair, Sullivan finds himself howling with laughter watching a Mickey Mouse cartoon in a Southern church.

The title references Jonathan Swift's *Gulliver's Travels*, another journey of self-discovery, and the name of author "Sinclair Beckstein" is an amalgam of Upton Sinclair, Sinclair Lewis and John Steinbeck, known for their socially conscious fiction.

Preston Sturges sums up his theme in the last reel, when Sullivan realizes, "There's a lot to be said for making people laugh...Do you know, that's all some people have?"

On the Granger Movie Gauge of 1 to 10, *Sullivan's Travels* is an ironic, timeless 10, satirizing the perennial conflict between art and commerce.

Talk to Her (SPC) (Hable con ella--Spanish) (2002)

After seeing this extraordinary Pedro Almodovar film, you may wonder why it was not eligible for an Academy Award as Best Foreign Language Film. That's because Spain chose to submit *Mondays in the Sun* as its national candidate for Oscar consideration, which is too bad.

The tender tragic comedy opens with a dancer careening like a sleepwalker across a stage littered with chairs while her partner rushes to clear these obstacles from her path. They're performers but in the audience are two men: Marco (Dario Grandinetti), a travel writer who is weeping openly, and Benigno (Javier Camara), an instinctively compassionate nurse who is moved by the journalist's tears. They then meet at a private clinic outside Madrid where the psychopathic Benigno is obsessively devoted to one patient—Alicia (Leonor Watling), a lovely, young dancer who's in a coma after a car accident—and Marco keeps a vigil over his lover, Lydia (Rosario Flores), a comatose matador.

The men develop a friendship, fueled by grief, loneliness and despair. The title comes from Benigno's advice to Marco about continuing his efforts to remain intimate and to communicate. Both actors are superb and Geraldine Chaplin scores in a supporting role as Alicia's ballet teacher. Pedro Almodovar, who delved into the female psyche with *Women on the Verge of a Nervous Breakdown* and *All About My Mother,* now reveals an unexpected moral ambiguity hidden deep within the emotional lives and needs of men. Plus, he continues his penchant for the surreal with a clever allegory: a silent, black-and-white film-within-a-film, *Shrinking Lover*.

On the Granger Movie Gauge of 1 to 10, *Talk to Her* is a complex, amusing, insightful 10. In Spanish with English subtitles, it's not to be missed.

There Will Be Blood (Paramount Vantage) (2007)

"**I** hate most people. My goal is to earn enough money so that I can get away from everyone," states taciturn Daniel Plainview (Daniel Day-Lewis) in Paul Thomas Anderson's strangely mesmerizing character-study of a ruthless, misanthropic oilman doggedly building an empire in early 20th-century California.

Based on the first 150 pages of Upton Sinclair's muckraking novel *Oil!*, the sprawling historical saga follows Plainview and his adopted son H.W. (Dillon Freasier) as they wheel-and-deal unsuspecting homesteaders out of their land rights, pursuing a plan to construct an oil pipeline to the Pacific Ocean from a rural enclave called Little Boston, near what is now Los Angeles.

Running roughshod over their competitors, they find an immovable obstacle in Eli Sunday (Paul Dano), an avaricious young evangelist who is as ambitious and unscrupulous as they are – only his goal is building the revivalist Church of the Third Revelation.

Delivering a powerful, Oscar-caliber performance, Daniel Day-Lewis embodies the driving force of the determined entrepreneur, as he, literally and figuratively, trounces all opposition, even banishing his son when the boy goes deaf after an accident. As his spiteful, Bible-thumping, mirror-image adversary, Paul Dano matches Day-Lewis' ferocious intensity.

Filmed around Marfa, Texas, where both *Giant* and *No Country for Old Men* were shot, P.T. Anderson's daring, adventurous storytelling process often unfolds without spoken dialogue, utilizing Robert Elswit's spectacular cinematography, Jack Fisk's brilliant production design and Radiohead guitarist Jonny Greenwood's evocative, dissonant score.

This epic concept is quite a departure from director/screenwriter Anderson's previous films - *Punch-Drunk Love, Magnolia, Boogie Nights*, and *Hard Eight*. He emerges as one of the most exciting filmmakers of this decade.

On the Granger Movie Gauge of 1 to 10, *There Will Be Blood* gushes to an astonishing, enthralling 10.

Three Colors: Blue, White, Red
(MK2 Productions) (1993, 1994)

I n this elliptical trilogy, celebrated Polish filmmaker Krzysztof Kieslowski collaborated with screenwriter Krzysztof Piesiewicz to create one of the most internationally influential, persuasive cinematic cycles.

Set in Paris, Warsaw, and Geneva, interconnected characters find themselves experiencing love and loss. The titles allude to the colors of the French flag, representing the aspirations of the French revolution: liberty, equality, fraternity. But they have little to do with either patriotism or national identity. Instead, they're about morality, reaching beyond national borders to become a portrait of Europe after the collapse of Communism.

In the deliberately paced *Blue* (1993), Juliette Binoche plays the sole survivor of the car crash that killed her composer husband and young daughter. Devastated, she tries to exorcize grief and deceit but the music she's trying to suppress eventually unlocks her reawakening.

In the wickedly satiric *White*, Zbigniew Zamachowski plays a gentle Polish immigrant living in France whose cruel wife (July Delpy) sues for divorce because he's impotent. Humiliated and determined to get revenge, he returns to Poland, where capitalism has created a country of cold opportunists.

In *Red*, a meditation on fate and chance, Irene Jacob plays a runway model who befriends a bitter, reclusive, retired judge (Jean-Louis Trintignant), who eavesdrops on his neighbors' phone calls. Together, they find friendship, forgiveness and redemption, as a young judge (Jean-Pierre Lorit) dates a neighbor of the old judge.

All three were conceived with story consultants Agnieszka Holland and Stawomir Idziak with musical scores by Zbigniew Preisner. Kieslowski noted in an interview at Oxford University: "The words (liberte, egalite, fraternite) are French because the money (to fund the films) is French. If the money had been of a different nationality, we would have titled (them) differently, or they might have had a different cultural connection. But the films would probably have been the same." Kieslowski held a firm conviction that one should depict subject matters and situations that link, not divide people, noting "If culture is capable of anything, then it is finding that which unites us all...Feelings are what link people together, because the word 'love' has the same meaning for everybody. Or 'fear,' or 'suffering.'"

On the Granger Movie Gauge of 1 to 10, *Three Colors: Blue, White, Red* is a powerful, sensually intoxicating 10. All three have been released on DVD, along with insightful commentaries.

Toy Story (Series) (Walt Disney) (1999-2010)
Toy Story 3

It's been 15 years since Woody, Buzz and the gang emerged in the *Toy Story* and 11 years since the first sequel. Now Disney/Pixar has come up with a third episode that's bigger (3-D!), perhaps cleverer and certainly delightful.

Opening with a rootin' tootin' action, screenwriter Michael Arndt (Oscar winner for *Little Miss Sunshine*) and director Lee Unkrich (co-director of *Toy Story 2, Monsters Inc,* and *Finding Nemo*) create a traumatic dilemma for the beloved characters.

Eighteen-year-old Andy (John Morris) is off to college and his mom (Laurie Metcalf) has told him to clean up his bedroom and sort his stuff. But instead of heading for attic storage, the outgrown toys wind up at Sunnyside Daycare Center. At first, Hamm the pink piggybank (John Ratzenberger), Jessie the cowgirl (Joan Cusack), Mr. & Mrs. Potato Head (Don Rickles, Estelle Harris), Slinky Dog (Brian Clark) and Rex the Dinosaur (Wallace Shawn) are excited. They're going to be played with! And Andy's sister Molly's discarded Barbie (Jodi Benson) finds bachelor Ken (Michael Keaton) with his dream house. But then reality dawns: the screaming horde of terrorizing toddlers seems set on abuse and destruction. And Lots-o'-Huggin' (Ned Beatty), a strawberry-scented pink plush bear, rules like a dictator.

Their only friend is Bonnie (Emily Hahn), the daughter of a daycare worker, who introduces a lederhosen-wearing hedgehog, Mr. Pricklepants (Timothy Dalton), along with Trixie the Triceratops (Kristen Schaal), Buttercup the unicorn (Jeff Garlin), doll Dolly (Bonnie Hunt) Peas-in-a-Pod and others. So Sheriff Woody (Tom Hanks) and Buzz Lightyear (Tim Allen) – who accidentally gets switched to Spanish mode – must devise a daring prison break to get back where they belong, to be passed along to another generation.

As always with Pixar, the animation is visually glorious and Randy Newman's music adds yet another dimension to the poignant humor and adventure.

On the Granger Movie Gauge of 1 to 10, *Toy Story 3* is a nostalgic 10, a loving, heartfelt treat for the kid in all of us. *Toy Story* may be the most treasured animated trilogy of all time.

Toy Story 2

Among our many blessings this Thanksgiving, let us be thankful for the astonishing, fun-filled *Toy Story* 2, the best animated comedy sequel ever made. This magical, incredibly inventive mix of action and humor continues, right where it left off, with the gang ready to play in Andy's bedroom. Only, when Andy goes off to Cowboy Camp, Woody gets left behind and is kidnapped by the greedy owner of Al's Toy Barn. It seems Woody's a highly valuable collectible from a 1950s TV show called Woody's Roundup.

At Al's place, Woody meets another family from his illustrious past – Jessie, the cowgirl; Bullseye, the horse; and Stinky Pete, the Prospector. But, back in Andy's house, Buzz Lightyear has recruited Mr. Potato Head, Slinky Dog, Rex and Hamm for a rescue mission. Can his pals find Woody before Andy comes home? And, will Woody want to come back to Andy's bedroom now that he's discovered he's a prized museum piece?

The original *Toy Story* was an international sensation, the third highest grossing animated film of all time—behind *The Lion King* and *Aladdin*. Originally planned as a direct-to-video release, this adventurous sequel reunites the same creative team, including Pixar's John Lasseter and Andrew Stanton, along with Tom Hanks, Tim Allen, Don Rickles, Jim Varney, Wallace Shawn, John Ratzenberger and Annie Potts.

New voices are Wayne Knight, Kelsey Grammer, and Joan Cusack, plus Little Mermaid Jodi Benson as Barbie. Composer Randy Newman's "You've Got a Friend in Me" is reprised, along with new songs "Woody's Roundup" and "When She Loved Me," sung by Sarah McLachlan.

On the Granger Movie Gauge of 1 to 10, *Toy Story 2* is another knockout 10. Don't miss it—or, as Buzz Lightyear would say: "To infinity and beyond!"

Up (Disney/Pixar) (2009)

While Palais aficionados may have questioned the choice of Disney/Pixar's new, ultra-high-tech digital 3-D fantasy to open the Cannes Film Festival, no one's quibbling now.

Director/writer Pete Docter and co-director/writer Bob Peterson set up the backstory superbly, introducing the lifelong bond between Carl Fredericksen (voiced by Ed Asner) and his wife Ellie which began when they were children, entranced by a 1930s newsreel chronicling the exploits of eccentric explorer Charles Muntz (voiced by Christopher Plummer). Believing "adventure is out there," it was always Carl and Ellie's dream to visit Paradise Falls, deep in the rain forest of South America, where the chagrined Muntz retreated in his dirigible, "Spirit of Adventure," after one of his 'discoveries' was declared a fraud. But fate had other plans.

At 78, Carl has become a cantankerous widower who feels he has only one way 'out' when he's banished to a retirement village. A retired balloon seller, he fills thousands of balloons with helium, attaches them to his house and soars up, up and away, only to discover there's a stowaway: pesky eight-year old Russell (voiced by Jordan Nagai), a Wilderness Explorer Scout determined to earn his Elderly Assistance badge.

"I've never been in a floating house before," Russell marvels. Where they go, how they get there and what they discover is sheer delight.

With minimal dialogue, the inventive, action-filled narrative flows simply and seamlessly, delicately touching on bittersweet themes of love and loss, along with the idea of escape and the importance of relationships and emotional growth - with nods to *The Wizard of Oz, The Lost World, The Red Balloon*, and even *Fitzcarraldo*.

The poignant, underplayed characterizations are flawless and the finely-textured, visually brilliant animation is dazzling, particularly curmudgeonly Carl's square-jawed face, subtly reminiscent of Spencer Tracy.

On the Granger Movie Gauge of 1 to 10, *Up* lifts off with a high-spirited, towering 10. It's SO effective, in fact, that whether you view it in 3-D or 2-D, you and your family are in for a terrific, fun-filled ride.

Up in the Air (Paramount Pictures) (2009)

No other picture this year captures contemporary angst like this bittersweet tale of an emotionally alienated, rootless frequent flyer, a suave corporate executive who travels 322 days a year and considers VIP lounges and a seat in business class as home, confessing, "To know me is to fly with me."

Cynical Ryan Bingham (George Clooney) is a transitional expert or "termination engineer," which means he makes his living by firing other firms' employees, explaining "We are here to make limbo tolerable...This is an opportunity for rebirth."

En route to his prestige status goal of accumulating 10 million American Airlines miles, Bingham thrives on dispassionate downsizing, along with delivering "What's In Your Backpack?" motivational lectures, advocating shedding the weight of possessions and relationships and being unattached to anyone or anything. He even establishes an easy-going sexual relationship with a likeminded fellow traveler, Alex Goran (Vera Farmiga), who tells him, "Just think of me as you think of yourself, only with a vagina."

But then Natalie (Anna Kendrick), a twentysomething efficiency analyst, tries to sell his Omaha-based boss, Craig Gregory (Jason Bateman), on the money-saving concept of grounding Ryan and his cohorts by going "glocal", defined as global-turned-local, which translates into firing people via video-conferencing, rather than face-to-face. Sandwiched among business trips to Wichita, Kansas City, Des Moines, Tulsa, Detroit and Miami – with naïve Natalie tagging along – peripatetic Bingham has an obligation to attend the wedding of his younger sister (Melanie Lynskey) in Milwaukee, after which he must face an unexpected mid-life crisis.

Director Jason Reitman (*Juno, Thank You for Smoking*), working with writer Sheldon Turner in adapting Walter Kirn's novel, creates a perceptive, often surprising, fast-paced socio-economic satire, an existentialist tragic-comedy that perceptively taps into current anxieties and recession fears as devastated employees experience real-life layoffs; those are not bit actors, they're real victims of job loss.

George Clooney is terrific as the charismatic rogue with Vera Farmiga as his sexy counterpart.

On the Granger Movie Gauge of 1 to 10, *Up in the Air* is a timely, turbulent 10.

Vertigo (Paramount Pictures) (1958)

Perhaps Alfred Hitchcock's greatest visual masterpiece, this 1958 psychological thriller revolves around a retired San Francisco police detective, John "Scottie" Ferguson (James Stewart), suffering from acrophobia (fear of heights), who is hired as a private investigator by Gavin Elster (Tom Helmore) to follow his wife Madeleine (Kim Novak) whom he fears is suicidal.

Produced and directed by Hitchcock, the mind-boggling screenplay was written by Samuel Taylor and Alec Coppel, based on the French novel *D'Entre les Morts* by Pierre Boileau and Thomas Narcejac. Uncredited second unit cameraman Irmin Roberts, not cinematographer Robert Burks, created the in-camera special effect that's become known as a "contra-zoom shot," or "vertigo shot," which causes a distortion of the perspective. The background of a scene appears to change size while the main subject remains the same; since this optical illusion has no correlation to normal human perception, the result is mentally disorienting. And the spinning spirals in Saul Bass's geometric title sequence were created by avant-garde animator/filmmaker/musician John Whitney.

Prominent in Hitchcock films is what he called the "MacGuffin," a plot device that sets the narrative in motion and motivates the characters. In *Vertigo*, it's the plot itself. Since Scottie's vertigo obsession is primary, two-thirds through the movie, Hitchcock reveals the twist ending in order to highlight suspense over surprise. And the reincarnation theme is a red herring or device/diversion used to distract from the original idea.

While Hitchcock always envisioned James Stewart as Scottie, he originally wanted Vera Miles to play Madeleine, but she became pregnant and was, therefore, unavailable. Hitchcock's traditional cameo can be glimpsed approximately 11 minutes into the film, as he walks past Gavin Elster's shipyard, wearing a grey suit and carrying a small horn case. And California's real Spanish mission San Juan Bautista never had a bell tower; what's seen in the film was created by models and matte paintings.

Although it received two Oscar nominations for Best Art/Set Decoration and Best Sound, it won nothing. Yet, in 2012, it was voted the 2nd greatest film ever made (after *Citizen Kane*) in the *Sight and Sound* survey of international film critics. And Bernard Herrmann's "Love Theme from *Vertigo*" was used for an extended sequence in *The Artist* (2011).

On the Granger Movie Gauge of 1 to 10, *Vertigo* is a cynical yet profoundly touching 10, as each viewing increases the circular intensity.

Wall-E (Disney/Pixar) (2008)

What if mankind had to leave Earth and somebody forgot to turn off the last robot?

That's why – in the year 2700 – little WALL-E, a Waste Allocation Load Lifter: Earth-Class, is still trash-compacting. Day-after-day, he dutifully glides through the toxic, post-apocalyptic wasteland, sifting through junk, forming it into neat cubes and neatly piling the detritus into scrap-skyscrapers.

He's lonely with only a cockroach for company, but he's assembled a comfy home, filled with curious treasures, like Zippo lighters, Rubik's Cubes and an old VHS tape of the 1969 musical *Hello, Dolly!*

One day, he finds a little green sprout. And, soon after, the Spaceship Axiom lands, depositing EVE (Extra-terrestrial Vegetation Evaluator), a sleek, egg-shaped probe-droid searching for evidence that Earth is ready for re-colonization.

EVE so entrances WALL-E that he hitches a ride back with her, traveling out into a distant galaxy, where he teaches the spaceship's plump, pear-shaped, pampered passengers, who have been reclining indolently in high-tech deck chairs for 700 years, how to be human again.

Writer/director David Stanton's (*Finding Nemo*) Pixar animators are extraordinary, elegantly conveying complex thoughts, an intricate storyline and a wide range of emotions with minimal dialogue. With his sad binocular eyes and tank-tread feet, WALL-E is immediately endearing; his expressive, metallic speech comes via Ben Buritt, the sound designer who 'voiced' Chewbacca, R2D2, and *E.T.*

WALL-E's cautionary environmental message rings green and clear, triumphing over the rampant consumerism with great credit to Thomas Newman's musical score which is evocative, exuberant and self-explanatory, including the *Thus Spake Zarathustra* theme from Stanley Kubrick's classic *2001*.

On the Granger Movie Gauge of 1 to 10, *WALL-E* is a wistful, whimsical 10. It's a visionary, robotic romance.

War Horse (Disney/DreamWorks) (2011)

Joining beloved horse movies like *The Black Stallion, Black Beauty, Hidalgo, Secretariat, Seabiscuit,* and *National Velvet* is Steven Spielberg's epic, emotionally triumphant adaptation of Michael Morpurgo's 1982 novel *War Horse.*

Set in rural England and Europe during W.W. I, it begins as a colt is born in the Devon countryside and later purchased at auction by Ted Narracott (Peter Mullan), a drunk, foolhardy tenant-farmer. As his long-suffering wife (Emily Watson) points out, what they really need is a plow horse, not a thoroughbred; a sentiment echoed by their sneering, insensitive, overbearing landlord (David Thewlis).

But their teenage son Albert (Jeremy Irvine) falls in love with the bay with four white stockings and a white cross on his forehead, naming him Joey. Training him, Albert discovers that Joey's not only quick to learn but also has tremendous perseverance. When England goes to war with Germany, Joey's conscripted and turned over to Cavalry Capt. Nicholls (Tom Hiddleston).

Tenaciously determined to bring his cherished horse home, Albert enlists, only to discover that Joey's miraculous journey has taken him behind enemy lines, where he's sheltered by a French farmer (Niels Arestrup) and his granddaughter (Celine Buckens), before entrapment on a "no-man's-land" battleground. Historically, between one and two million British horses were sent to the front lines during W.W. I; only 65,000 or so came back.

Working from a nostalgic, melodramatic screenplay by Richard Curtis and Lee Hall, Spielberg surrounds himself with a stellar production staff, including cinematographer Janusz Kaminski, editor Michael Kahn and composer John Williams. To play Joey, 14 different horses were used by trainer Bobby Lovgren under strict supervision by the American Humane Association; only in portions of the barbed-wire sequence was an animatronic horse used.

In 2007, Nick Stafford's dramatization became a sensation on London's West End, presenting Joey as a fantastic, life-size puppet; the American theatrical version is still at Manhattan's Lincoln Center.

On the Granger Movie Gauge of 1 to 10, *War Horse* is a stirring, sentimental, tear-jerking 10, joining Spielberg's *Saving Private Ryan* and *Schindler's List* in a universal plea for peace.

Waste Land (Arthouse Films) (2010)

Set at Jardim Gramacho, a massive outdoor garbage dump on the outskirts of Rio de Janiero, Lucy Walker's fascinating Portuguese/English documentary profiles Vik Muniz, a successful Sao Paulo-born, Brooklyn-based artist who is internationally recognized for recreating provocative projects like Leonardo da Vinci's *Last Supper* in unconventional mediums, like dirt, diamonds, sugar, string and chocolate syrup - then photographing the images to produce large constructions.

For this project, Muniz photographed recyclable materials pickers ("catadores") working at the landfill and then created large collages out of the debris they collected. His *Pictures of Garbage Series* at MAM in Rio was second only to Picasso in attendance records. Eventually, Muniz donated $300,000 from the monumental art sale to the workers so they could purchase equipment and build a resource center.

One particular laborer, Tiao Santos, was overwhelmed when he realized the monetary value ($50,000) placed in London on *Marat/Sabastio,* a painting of him which recreates the image of the *Death of Marat*, a French Revolutionary leader whose politics and philosophy motivated him. Having educated himself by reading discarded books, Santos subsequently organized the 2,500 workers into the Association of Pickers of Jardim Gramacho, noting that he was also inspired by the writings of Niccolo Machiavelli because he sees similarities between the social and political instability in Florence in the 16th century and the current situation in Brazil.

Regarding conservation, as one picker put it, "One can is of great importance. Because 99 is not 100, and that single one will make the difference."

Oscar-nominated for Best Documentary Feature in 2011, on the Granger Movie Gauge of 1 to 10, *Waste Land* is a sensitive, thought-provoking 10, illustrating the transformative power of art.

Update: Jardim Gramacho closed in June, 2012, just in time for the Rio+20 UN environmental conference. The landfill will be transformed into a park, but the government's waste department, Companhia Municipal de Limpeza urbana (COMLURB) estimates that it will take at least 15 years for the land to fully recover. It has been reported that compensation money will be awarded to some of the workers there, but disputes have arisen as to how many are eligible.

The Way We Were (Columbia Pictures) (1973)

This 1973 romantic melodrama about missed opportunities is the ultimate chick flick, marking the first and only time that equally charismatic Barbra Streisand and Robert Redford ever appeared in a film together.

Serious Katie Morosky (Streisand) is an outspoken, left-wing, Jewish New Yorker, while fun-loving Hubbell Gardiner (Redford) is a blue-eyed, blond, jock from Virginia. She's an agitator; he's politically apathetic. With the irresistible attraction of opposites, these ill-fated lovers meet and marry. Determined that Hubbell hone his writing talent, they movie to California when he does the screen adaptation of a novel he's written. When Hollywood's commercial demands destroy him, disillusioned Katie divorces files for divorce. Both eventually find more suitable mates before they meet by chance once again —in front of New York's Plaza Hotel - and realize that they can never return to the past.

Commissioned by producer Ray Stark (who was married to comedian Fanny Brice's daughter), Arthur Laurents wrote the script, modeling it on a Cornell classmate, a member of the Young Communist League named Fanny Price, and his own experiences with Sen. Joe McCarthy's House Un-American Activities Committee. Sensitive director Sydney Pollack deliberately emphasized how sweet and sad memories can be. And with incredible tact and acuity, cinematographer Harry Stradling Jr. managed to satisfy both Redford's and Streisand's stipulations that—in close-ups—they both be photographed on their 'left' side.

As the film begins, there are two indelible flashbacks: at the Manhattan nightclub El Morocco, Katie spots handsome Hubbell seated at the bar, dressed in his navy whites – fast asleep, and then, when this insecure, neurotic, unglamorous woman seduces the idealized man of her dreams, she realizes he's so drunk that he'll never remember he made love to her.

Nominated for six Academy Awards, it won two – for music. Although Streisand reportedly loathed Alan and Marilyn Bergman's original lyrics, Marvin Hamlisch's title song won an Oscar and turned out to be Streisand's #1 hit single for an entire year. While sequels were commissioned and considered, none ever came to fruition. So when Redford was introduced by Streisand at the 2002 Oscars and given an honorary Lifetime Achievement Award, he looked at her, quipping, "I guess this is a sequel, huh, Bab?"

On the Granger Movie Gauge of 1 to 10, *The Way We Were* is a teary 10, an admittedly schmaltzy weeper.

Whale Rider (Newmarket Films) (2002)

If you enjoyed how John Sayles evoked the Irish essence in *The Secret of Roan Inish*, don't miss Niki Caro's contemporary fable set in New Zealand's traditionally patrilineal Maori culture.

Paikea (Keisha Castle-Hughes), called Pai, is the twelve-year-old granddaughter of Koro (Rawiri Paratene), leader of the Whangara tribe, who resents her very existence. Her still-born fraternal twin was to have continued Koro's bloodline which can be traced back to the first aboriginal inhabitants—and legend has it that these ancestors were borne to their island home on the back of a whale. Not only did Pai survive the difficult birth that killed her mother and brother but her father (Cliff Curtis) then deserted the family for a career as an artist in Germany, returning to visit only occasionally.

So the only nurturing that Pai has received during her short lifetime is from her grandmother Nanny Flowers (Vicky Haughton). Nevertheless, she is resourceful and skilled in handling weapons, diving and singing tribal chants. Above all, she is determined to take her rightful place within the tribe – a phenomenon that occurs only after the sacred whales beach themselves on the shore near their village until Pai comes to their rescue.

Adapting Witi Ihimaera's 1987 novel, screenwriter/director Niki Caro and cinematographer Leon Narbey have created a haunting, dreamlike, artistic gem, particularly when Pai sings an ancient tribal song to a dark ocean. And beautiful Keisha Castle-Hughes is a spunky young charmer with a gravity reminiscent of Anna Paquin in *The Piano*.

On the Granger Movie Gauge of 1 to 10, *Whale Rider* is a mysterious, mythic 9. But—be warned—that, while the film is in English, some of the thick accents are difficult to decipher.

The Wicker Man (British Lion) (1973)

Described by the film magazine *Cinefantastique* as "The *Citizen Kane* of Horror Movies," this 1973 genre-defying musical mystery thriller, directed by Robin Hardy and written by Anthony Shaffer, was inspired by David Pinner's 1967 novel *Ritual*, in which Police Sergeant Neil Howie (Edward Woodward) visits the isolated Scottish island of Summerisle in search of a missing girl whom the locals claim never existed.

A chaste bachelor and devout Christian, righteous Howie is appalled to discover that the island's secluded inhabitants practice a form of paganism, worshipping the ancestral Celtic gods by offering sacrifices to them. Rooming at an inn, he's seductively approached by the landlord's lascivious daughter Willow (Brett Ekland). But he's determined to investigate a curious series of photographs celebrating the annual harvest festival, which lead him to contact the community's leader, Laird (Lord) Summerisle (Christopher Lee), who explains the ancient rituals, subtly preparing him for what will become an ominous and horrifying cultural confrontation.

The haunting image of the titular wicker man was taken from Julius Caesar's observations of how primitive tribes executed their most serious criminals by burning them alive in a huge, human-shaped sculpture that was woven of twigs. That was reinforced by anthropologist James Frazer's comprehensive study of mythology and religion *The Golden Bough*.

Shot with great authenticity on location in rural Scotland, it's become a cult classic, despite the loss of the original negative and outtakes that were stored in the Shepperton studios vault and accidentally discarded. Fortunately, a print had been sent to Hollywood producer Roger Corman, who enabled Robin Hardy and producer Peter Snell to reconstruct the film in its erotic entirety.

"The concept of film fantastique is based on the idea that you can incorporate ordinary life – songs, music, humor – where, underneath, something sinister lurks," explains Robin Hardy.

While Neil LaBute's wretched 2006 American remake, starring Nicolas Cage and Ellen Burstyn, is best forgotten, Hardy made a spiritual sequel, *The Wicker Tree* (2011), and is developing *The Wrath of the Gods*, to complete his thematic trilogy.

On the Granger Movie Gauge of 1 to 10, *The Wicker Man* is an inscrutable 8, dealing with paganism in the modern world.

Wild Tales (Sony Pictures Classics) (Spanish) (2014)

Opening with one of the shortest and most amusing segments, Argentinean filmmaker Damian Szifron's unconventional anthology is built around the psychological concept of revenge.

Pasternak deals with a fateful encounter on a plane, as a suave music critic (Dario Grandinetti) begins a conversation with a beautiful model (Maria Marull), seated across the aisle. Within moments, they discover they're not the only people in business class with a connection to the model's ex-boyfriend, Gabriel Pasternak. Think *Twilight Zone*.

Rats revolves around a waitress (Julieta Zylbergberg) in a roadside diner who discovers that her only customer (Cesar Bordon) is the loan shark who drove her father to suicide. When the ex-con cook (Rita Cortese) learns the truth, retribution seems inevitable.

As the cautionary *Road to Hell* begins, a rich, arrogant businessman (Leonardo Sbarglia) is driving his shiny, new Audi, rudely giving the finger to a redneck (Walter Donado) in an old Peugeot. Then when the Audi gets a flat tire, road rage takes over.

In "Bombita," a Buenos Aires demolition engineer (Ricardo Darin), whose car keeps getting towed in streets that don't have NO PARKING signs, destroys his career and his marriage.

The Deal finds a wealthy patriarch (Oscar Martinez) paying his gardener (German de Silva) to take the blame for a hit-and-run accident caused by his spoiled son (Alan Dalcz).

Finally, *Til Death Do Us Part* occurs during a festive wedding reception in which the bride (Erica Rivas) discovers that the groom (Diego Gentile) is cheating on her.

Writer/director Damian Szifron confidently links these diverse short stories around the same behavioral theme: what happens when people are pushed to the edge. It's an intriguing and compelling concept.

On the Granger Movie Gauge of 1 to 10, *Wild Tales* is an inventive 9, one of the most entertaining Foreign Language films of 2014.

The Wizard of Oz (M.G.M.) (1939)

On May 1, 1938, M.G.M. embarked on production #1060, the screen adaptation of L. Frank Baum's books budgeted at a then-astounding $3,700,000. Sixteen-year-old Judy Garland was cast as Dorothy, the orphan girl from Kansas who maintains "There's no place like home", with Ray Bolger as the Scarecrow, Jack Haley as the Tin Man, Bert Lahr as the Cowardly Lion, Billie Burke as Glinda the Good, Frank Morgan as Professor Marvel, a former Cleveland schoolteacher named Margaret Hamilton as the Wicked Witch of the West, and 124 midgets (hypo-pituitary dwarfs), ranging in size from 2'3" to 4'8", playing Munchkins. A Cairn terrier named Terry played Toto.

In charge of the challenging production was producer Arthur Freed, who not only signed Harold Arlen and E.Y. "Yip" Harburg to write the music but also coordinated the contributions of costumer Adrian and gifted art directors Cedric Gibbons, Bill Horning, and Jack Martin Smith under director Victor Fleming.

The opening and closing scenes in Kansas were shot in sepia tint, while the Oz segment was photographed in Technicolor, a relatively new process devised by Dr. Henry Kalmus. The tornado was the most difficult and costly of A. Arnold (Buddy) Gillespie's inventive special effects.

For the memorable Horse of a Different Color sequence, six white horses were sponged down with green, blue, orange, red, yellow, and violet Jell-O powder. To photograph the Deadly Poppy Field, the first dolly track was laid, allowing the camera to move very low to the ground. And to depict the Witch's melting, Ms. Hamilton stood atop a hydraulic elevator with her cloak fastened to the floor as dry-ice vapors gave the illusion of melting, leaving nothing on the stage but her costume.

Ironically, the song "Over the Rainbow" was almost eliminated because, during sneak previews, studio bosses felt its wistful theme was above children's heads.

On the Granger Movie Gauge of 1 to 10, *The Wizard of Oz* is a magical, tuneful 10, becoming an integral part of the American cultural fabric perhaps because it's shown so often on television.

The World's Fastest Indian (Magnolia Films) (2005)

Anthony Hopkins channels Steve McQueen as an indomitable motorcycle racer who is determined to enter his 1920 Indian Twin Scout in competition at Utah's Bonneville Salt Flats.

An eccentric car mechanic in Invercargill, a small coastal town in New Zealand, seventy-two-year-old Burt Munro (Hopkins) has a dream: setting the world's land-speed record. He's modified his red, rocket-shaped antique motorbike to operate at more than 200 m.p.h., observing that at that speed, "You live more in five minutes than most people live in a lifetime."

Ever the optimist, his enthusiasm is contagious, even though his health is precarious and his unstable relic has no brakes. Working as a galley cook on a small freighter from New Zealand to Los Angeles, then driving to Utah, he ingeniously makes friends along the way, including an amiable transvestite (Chris Williams), a Salvadoran used-car salesman (Paul Rodriguez), a lonely widow (Diane Ladd) with welding equipment, a helpful hitch-hiking soldier (Patrick Flueger) and an influential competitor (Christopher Kennedy Lawford) who persuades skeptical officials to "bend" the rules to allow Munro to qualify for the annual "Speed Week" competition.

Writer/director Roger Donaldson (*The Recruit*), who made a '70s TV documentary (*Offerings to the God of Speed*) about the legendary, real-life Burt Munro (1899-1978), scores with versatile, adventuresome Anthony Hopkins, whose sly, warm, quirky charm elevates this cheery, complex curmudgeon's journey to an idiosyncratic, endearing, spiritual odyssey.

On the Granger Movie Gauge of 1 to 10, *The World's Fastest Indian* accelerates to an uplifting, intrepid 9, hitting "feel good" on all cylinders. As Munro puts it, "Danger is the spice of life."

Youth (Fox Searchlight Pictures) (2015)

Evoking memories of Federico Fellini's *8 ½*, Italy's Paolo Sorrentino, who won a Foreign Language Film Oscar for *The Great Beauty* (2013), uses imagery as an integral part of the story.

Set in a sumptuous Alpine spa, the rambling plot revolves around Fred Ballinger (Michael Caine), a retired British composer/conductor, and his longtime pal, American screenwriter/director Mick Boyle (Harvey Keitel).

Fred is accompanied by his neurotic daughter, Lena (Rachel Weisz), while Mick struggles with his next script, attended by several sycophants. Relationships get strained when Lena's feckless husband (Ed Stoppard), who happens to be Mick's son, leaves her for sexy British pop star Paloma Faith (playing herself).

As Fred and Mick playfully ponder their prostates, as well as their respective legacies, and ruminate about their womanizing pasts, they're surrounded by attentive staff and other guests.

There's Jimmy Tree (Paul Dano), a serious, self-absorbed actor, preparing for an unnerving role; an obese former soccer star (Roly Serrano); a lovelorn mountaineering instructor (Robert Seethaler); an elegant couple who always dine alone, never speaking to one another; and voluptuous Miss Universe (Madalina Ghenea), who strolls into the warm, sun-dappled pool unabashedly nude.

When Queen Elizabeth II's emissary (Alex Macqueen) arrives, he invites Fred to conduct a Royal Concert of *Simple Songs*, an early composition which triggers more melancholy memories than he can handle. Then Mick is stunned by a disquieting visit from his eccentric cinematic muse, bitter Brenda Morel (Jane Fonda).

FYI: the idyllic Swiss hotel is actually Berghotel Schatzalp, near Davos, which inspired Thomas Mann's *The Magic Mountain*.

Working with a multitude of interacting characters and unpredictable ideas, Paolo Sorrentino and his cinematographer, Luca Bigazzi, relish the lush, rhythmic visuality, while New York-based post-Minimalist composer David Lang contributes an evocative score – as both Caine and Keitel deliver subtle, multi-layered performances, among the best of their respective careers.

On the Granger Movie Gauge of 1 to 10, *Youth* is an idiosyncratic, exquisite 8, an empathetic meditation on the human spirit.

Zootopia (Walt Disney Animation Studio) (2016)

Is it too early for a 2017 Academy Awards prediction? *Zootopia* will not only be nominated but, unless Pixar tops it in the next few months, the Mouse House will win Oscar gold for Best Animated Feature.

In the modern metropolis of Zootopia, anthropomorphic mammals have evolved beyond their primitive predator/prey status, each species living peacefully within its own appropriate habitat, like Sahara Square, Tundratown, Rain Forest and Little Rodentia.

Plucky Judy Hopps (voiced by Ginnifer Goodwin) is an idealistic rabbit who is not content to work on her family's carrot farm with her 225 siblings. When a bullying, red-furred fox bothers her classmates, she shows an early aptitude for conflict management, becoming the first bunny to enroll in Zootopia's Police Academy.

Despite graduating at the top of her class, Bogo (voiced by Idris Elba), her gruff Cape buffalo boss, makes tiny Judy a lowly meter-maid while larger, more experienced officers investigate an intriguing case involving 14 missing mammals.

Protesting, "I'm not just some token bunny," rookie Judy becomes obsessively determined to write more parking-violation tickets than anyone ever before.

On-duty, she spies wily Nick Wilde (voiced by Jason Bateman), a hustling, fast-talking fox who becomes her frenemy as they become entangled in the missing mammal mystery.

Some of the funniest, most inventive sequences visit the Department of Motor Vehicles, staffed by slow-moving sloths, and the hideaway of a Godfather-like gangster, Mr. Big (Maurice LaMarche), plus a musical interval with pop star Gazelle (voiced by Shakira) warbling "Try Everything."

Deftly directed by Bryon Howard (*Tangled*), Rich Moore (*Wreck-It Ralph*) and Jared Bush, who share scripting credit with several others, it's an imaginatively amusing, subversively relevant, heartfelt parable/police procedural about tolerance and acceptance. Children will enjoy the action-packed comedy, while adults will find plenty of topics, like diversity, prejudice and stereotyping ("dumb bunny," "sly fox"), to discuss on the way home.

On the Granger Movie Gauge of 1 to 10, *Zootopia* is an intrepid 10, summed up by Judy's appeal, "No matter what type of animal you are, change starts with you."

ABOUT THE AUTHOR

Susan Granger was born into a film-business family—her father was director and producer S. Sylvan Simon whose credits include *Son of Lassie, Bud Abbott and Lou Costello in Hollywood,* and *Born Yesterday*—and raised in Hollywood, she appeared as a child actress in movies with Abbott & Costello, Red Skelton, Lucille Ball, and Lassie.

After her father died at just 41 while preparing *From Here to Eternity*, her mother later remarried. Her stepfather, Armand Deutsch, was also in the industry: MGM producer whose credits included *The Magnificent Yankee* (1950).

Susan studied journalism with Pierre Salinger at Mills College and graduated with highest honors in journalism with a B.A. from the University of Pennsylvania.

For more than 25 years, she has been an on-air television and radio commentator and entertainment critic. Her commentaries, reviews, and interviews are distributed around the world by SSG Syndicate. Susan is also the film critic for the monthly magazine, *Video Librarian*.

For more on Susan's background, or to book her as a speaker, go to her main website: http://www.susangranger.com

Susan Granger with Red Skelton on the
set of *The Fuller Brush Man*

CPSIA information can be obtained
at www.ICGtesting.com
Printed in the USA
LVOW04s1606250117
522153LV00005B/179/P